HARRIET JACOBS

HARRIET JACOBS

⊰ A PLAY ⊱

LYDIA R. DIAMOND

Foreword by Megan Sandberg-Zakian with Jean Fagan Yellin

Inspired by *Incidents in the Life of a Slave Girl* by Harriet Jacobs

NORTHWESTERN UNIVERSITY PRESS

EVANSTON, ILLINOIS

Northwestern University Press
www.nupress.northwestern.edu
Copyright © 2011 by Lydia R. Diamond.
Published 2011 by Northwestern University Press. All rights reserved.

Printed in the United States of America

10 9 8 7 6 5 4 3 2 1

LIBRARY OF CONGRESS
CATALOGING-IN-PUBLICATION DATA

Diamond, Lydia R., 1969–
    Harriet Jacobs : a play / Lydia R. Diamond ; foreword by Megan Sandberg-Zakian with Jean Fagan Yellin.
        p. cm.
    "Inspired by Incidents in the Life of a Slave Girl by Harriet Jacobs."
    ISBN-13: 978-0-8101-2716-6 (pbk. : alk. paper)
    ISBN-10: 0-8101-2716-4 (pbk. : alk. paper)
    1. Jacobs, Harriet A. (Harriet Ann), 1813–1897—Drama. 2. Slavery—United States—Drama. 3. Women slaves—United States—Drama. 4. Jacobs, Harriet A. (Harriet Ann), 1813–1897. I. Title.
    PS3604.I1557H37 2011
    812'.6—dc22

                                    2011000448

∞ The paper used in this publication meets the minimum requirements of the American National Standard for Information Sciences—Permanence of Paper for Printed Library Materials, ANSI Z39.48-1992.

CONTENTS

FOREWORD

Slightly Beyond Knowing:
The Neo-Utopian Vision of Harriet Jacobs

Megan Sandberg-Zakian with Jean Fagan Yellin

In 1861, a book appeared in Boston whose title page named neither an author nor a publisher. It read, *Incidents in the Life of a Slave Girl, Written by Herself, Edited by L. Maria Child.* The first line of the author's preface declared, "Reader, be assured this narrative is no fiction," and claimed that other than disguising the names of people and places (mostly, the author gently implied, to protect the guilty), the incredible tale was "strictly true." This preface was signed "Linda Brent," the pseudonym of the "slave girl" of the title. An editor's introduction by Child, a prominent author and White abolitionist, underscored these claims and vouched for "Linda's" reliability.

The "Linda" of *Incidents* was actually a middle-aged resident of Cornwall, New York, named Harriet Jacobs, who had been held a slave in Edenton, North Carolina, before fleeing to the North nearly twenty years earlier, at age twenty-nine. Jacobs's brother, John, had arrived in the North before his sister and was well known in the abolitionist community, at one time lecturing alongside Frederick Douglass. Harriet, too, had become part of this community. In her correspondence with notable reformers of the time, both Black and White, Jacobs sometimes even signed "Linda" alongside her own name.

Somehow, however, in spite of her relatively high profile during her lifetime, it did not take long for Harriet Jacobs to be all but erased from the pages of history. The style of *Incidents* is unique and its content is so astonishing that literary and historical scholars came to doubt Jacobs's authorship—and even her existence. By the middle of the twentieth century, it was generally held that the book was another novel by Lydia Maria Child. Luckily, some of Child's correspondence concerning the manuscript was discovered by Dr. Jean Fagan Yellin, a professor at Pace University. Yellin's unflagging scholarship snatched Jacobs from the abyss of obscurity, unearthing the evidence of her authorship and affirming the accuracy of most of the events she described. Yellin did not stop with two editions of *Incidents* (reclassified by the Library of Congress to indicate Jacobs as the author). She followed the trail of Jacobs's exceptional life past the time of the book's conclusion, publishing a meticulous and engaging biography in 2004, *Harriet Jacobs: A Life.*

With Jacobs definitively established as the narrative's author and her book as an autobiography, we are left to wonder what made this document so unbelievable. Certainly Jacobs's story itself is extraordinary. The events of her life in slavery differ in striking ways from other information we have about the lives of female slaves: learning to read at a young age; rejecting the sexual advances of her master, Dr. James Norcom; entering into a consensual affair with an unmarried White slave owner with whom she conceived two children; and escaping from Norcom only to remain right under his nose—hidden in a crawl space under the roof of her grandmother's porch for seven long years. The events of her life after slavery seem no less extraordinary. "We don't know of any woman who was a slave in the South, a fugitive in the South and the North, who wrote a slave narrative and then went back down South to do relief work and establish a school," Yellin pointed out. "And she wrote about it in the Northern press to publicize the condition of the Black refugees from slavery. We just didn't have that story before, and now we do." The last point seems particularly salient: we did not have that story before now. It is therefore conceivable, even probable, that there are other stories which we still "just don't have"—some that may bear a similarity to Jacobs's and some that may be extraordinary in different, unprecedented ways.

Yellin recently published *The Harriet Jacobs Family Papers,* the first scholarly edition of the papers of a Black woman held in slavery.

That long-overdue volume serves as a reminder that our most familiar stories about Black women in slavery are not in their own voices—in sharp contrast to those of both Black men and White women of the same era. Harriet Beecher Stowe, author of perhaps the most influential abolitionist text, *Uncle Tom's Cabin*, was a White woman. Sojourner Truth and Harriet Tubman, female heroes of the slavery struggle, were illiterate; although their stories were transcribed, they were not able to create a written record of their own making. While Frederick Douglass and other men who had been held in slavery touched on the experiences of their female friends and relatives, none was able to be as frank about the experiences of women in the slaveholding South—both Black and White—as Jacobs. In particular, Jacobs describes unconscionable sexual practices that thrived under chattel slavery: the ubiquity of the rape of slaves at the hands of their masters, including the rape of children, and the unnatural result of such an act—a parent owning, and profiting from the sale of, his own offspring. She writes of the spread of this perverted sexual culture to the wives and children of slaveholders, demonstrating the incompatibility of the system of slavery with the era's emphasis on feminine purity and virtue.

Yellin's documentation of Jacobs's extensive correspondence reveals that Jacobs's embarrassment about her own complicated sexual past nearly kept her from telling her story. "I had determined to let others think as they pleased, but my lips should be sealed and no one had a right to question me," she wrote to her Quaker friend Amy Post. "For this reason when I first came North I avoided the Antislavery people as much as possible because I felt that I could not be honest and tell the whole truth." In all likelihood, if it were not for Post's encouragement, even insistence, *Incidents* would never have been written, let alone published.

When Jacobs finally did decide to tell her story, she was not only a former "slave girl"—she was a mature woman who had lived for almost twenty years in several Northern cities, journeyed to Europe, and worked and corresponded with some of America's most prominent abolitionists. Her perspective was more expansive than that of many of her readers who may not have traveled or read as widely as she. She had had the chance to observe the response of Northern and European audiences to abolitionist arguments and to gauge her own rhetorical power through anonymous letters she sent to the editors of local newspapers.

Earlier, wanting to tell her story but doubting her ability to write effectively about her experiences, Jacobs had enlisted the aid of her prominent White friends Amy Post and Cornelia Willis to contact another White woman who she thought might be able to help—the day's most famous abolitionist writer, Harriet Beecher Stowe. When approached with the request to bring Jacobs's unusual life to the page, Stowe replied dismissively that she would be happy to incorporate an anecdote about Jacobs's story into her new book, *The Key to Uncle Tom's Cabin*. Incensed, Jacobs declared in a letter to Amy Post that her story "needed no romance" and finally began to write the book herself. Her comment about "romance" is notable, because *Incidents* is frequently cited as employing the sentimental tone of a popular Victorian romance novel in order to engage the sympathies of nineteenth-century female readers. Actually, its skillful mimicry of the genre was one of the factors that critics cited when expressing doubt about whether the book was, in fact, an autobiography. But if Jacobs had intended her story as a romantic novel, she could have taken advantage of Stowe's offer and spared herself the long hours writing in her employer's attic, late at night, after a full day of work.

Jacobs wanted her story to stand on its own. She clearly intended it to be more than a romantic account, and perhaps even more than a historical document to aid the cause of abolitionism. There is a detectable edge to both the romantic and abolitionist sentiments in her text. Over and over she reminds her readers that the nineteenth-century moral code is in direct conflict not only with the system of slavery but with the ubiquitous racism she finds in Northern states and with the compromised morality she experiences everywhere in her travels—even in her own soul. When she receives a letter in which her grandmother reports that old Master Norcom has died and expresses a hope that he has "made his peace with God," she cannot agree. "I cannot say, with truth, that the news of my old master's death softened my feelings towards him," she writes. "There are wrongs which even the grave does not bury. The man was odious to me while he lived, and his memory is odious now."

In the book *Utopia in Performance*, critic Jill Dolan suggests that some contemporary performance may have a "neo-utopian" vision—a perspective inverting the Romanticism inherent in old ideas of utopia, which clung to the idea of restoring the virtues of a foregone golden age. Neo-utopianism, on the other hand, is "romantic about the future—not about the past." Inherent in *Incidents* is this kind of neo-utopian vision. Perhaps this is what makes the narrative feel so far ahead of its time. Jacobs of course calls for abolition, but she also calls for human rights and humanity on multiple levels—she indicts everyone from her "kind" White lover (who is willing to treat his own children as property) to a Black preacher (whose warning that Jacobs may be condemned for her sexual history sentences her to years of shamed silence) to the liberal Northerners (who claim to oppose slavery while enforcing the harsh Fugitive Slave Laws) to even her beloved grandmother (who is sometimes blinded by her bouts of anxiety and religiosity). Jacobs's refusal to let anyone off the hook—least of all herself—is grounded in an implicit sense of faith, of possibility. We can *all* do better, she seems to be telling us—we *must* all do better.

Nearly 150 years after the publication of *Incidents in the Life of a Slave Girl*, interest in the text has surged. It is being read, taught, and studied extensively, and now performed, thanks to a stage adaptation by playwright Lydia R. Diamond. Jacobs finds a perfect collaborator in Diamond, whose interest in *Incidents* seems to lie not in its incidents, but in its neo-utopian vision. Diamond's play, *Harriet Jacobs*, places a version of the narrative of Jacobs's life alongside an inquiry into what we may think we already know about her life. This juxtaposition pointedly performs the question that artists and historians often ask in private but too rarely put at the center of their work: "Why are we telling this story?" The play does not answer this question, but it implies that if our goal is to learn from the past, we are not served by telling and retelling the same story, learning and relearning the same lesson. "You've heard about that," says Harriet in the play, after a gruesome description of the way slaves are treated on a plantation, "or at least something like it . . . This is not what I wish to tell you." Diamond's text, like Jacobs's, asks us to consider all the ways we *don't* understand history, all the ways we have become comfortable with one kind of narrative of slavery and, by extension, with one kind of narrative about race, class, gender, power, and privilege.

Jacobs and Diamond, both writing in times and places removed from the incidents they recount, share a keen understanding of the images their audiences have already absorbed of the institution of chattel slavery, and both attempt to use those images in the service of their particular goals. For example, Diamond has set some scenes of the play in a cotton field—though she was well aware that Jacobs lived in North Carolina, a state that grew not cotton, but tobacco and corn. Yet here—like Jacobs, who in describing the mistreatment of a slave, concludes, "These God-breathing machines are no more, in the sight of their masters, than the cotton they plant, or the horses they tend"—Diamond invokes cotton metaphorically as an easily recognized symbol of the labor of slaves in the American South. Diamond then goes on to treat the image of the cotton field in a series of surprising ways—a site for fantasy, beauty, and romantic games. When Diamond reintroduces a familiar role for the cotton field—as a site for a brutal beating by an overseer—it is thrown into stark relief against the lingering sense of beauty and possibility. While we might once have felt familiar, even comfortable, with the cotton field as a symbol of slavery, we are now experiencing the same image as unfamiliar, uncomfortable, unknown. "I promise that you may believe you have heard it, you may believe you know this," Harriet says in the play's opening moments, "and I suggest that it is slightly beyond knowing, because still, I hear the stories, I live the stories, and I do not yet understand."

In this most fundamental way, the play hews faithfully to the essence of Jacobs's life and work. To reach her audience, Diamond, like Jacobs, embroiders with the neo-utopian thread of image, metaphor, and emotional appeal. Each asks her audience to imagine (and reimagine) the experience of living inside the "peculiar institution" of slavery for Black and White Americans, men and women, free and slave, rich and poor. Each asks us to consider that, for those who lived its reality every day, slavery was difficult to comprehend, and that even now—or especially now—it remains "slightly beyond knowing."

Perhaps as we become more comfortable with the idea that some parts of our history are slightly beyond knowing, the more comfortable we can become with Jacobs's and Diamond's neo-utopian vision of America. They insist that we carry the past with us humbly, aware of its mysteries but not paralyzed by its weight, and not overwhelmed by its shadows—moved by romantic imaginings of our shared future rather than by imperfect recollections of our shared past.

A QUICK NOTE FROM THE PLAYWRIGHT

So, there's something I wish to tell you. Something I've learned while continually revising through many early rehearsals, workshops, and sessions with brilliant dramaturgs, friends, and colleagues.

Every time I enter a new rehearsal process I am taken by how incredibly emotionally challenging it is to inhabit the people, feelings, and customs of this obscene institution, slavery. This is what theater artists do, and while we're absolutely up to the task—because we have been trained to do our homework, be open, be present, be vulnerable, sensitive, and precise—it can still be daunting.

Through the writing of this piece, I have felt sometimes so utterly inadequate. How do I presume to honor this reality that my ancestors lived? How can I, a consumer of so many exoticized, romanticized, sanitized, infantilizing images of slavery, do justice to the portion of Harriet Jacobs's remarkable life that I wish to share with you?

And this is what I have learned. I am obligated to try. I'm a playwright and when there is a story to tell, I am compelled to tell it. I want Harriet Jacobs to exist, theatrically, alongside Anne Frank and Joan of Arc, because she deserves to. Because young and old, we need her.

This is also what I have learned. It is hard not to drown in the presumed misery of it all, before cracking the book open, before the houselights even come down.

When you read this play, act this play, direct or produce this play, try not to dwell only in the pain of it. Try, I think, to humbly acknowledge that we bring to it what we do, through the perspectives that we have, whether you agree that it is a slightly skewed perspective or not, and then put that aside and live in the present I've tried to create.

In her book, *Incidents in the Life of a Slave Girl*, Ms. Jacobs works to articulate to us the horrors of slavery. In my play, I work to articulate the psychological conundrum of trying to put words to that which is unspeakable. I work to celebrate the humanity that lived between and around the pain. I am aware that my ancestors, who were enslaved people, lived and cried, and loved and laughed, agitated and manipulated, more fully aware of their own predicament than we'll ever be, but always human and always with a will to live.

Honor, please, the humor in this play, where there is humor. Honor the burgeoning affections where they exist. The familial love where it lives. Try not to plod through it with a guilty, pained, apologetic, pitying, angry, contemporary sensibility—that's too easy. Let it live, please, from moment to moment, from laughs to tears, as we live life, walking through the murk of our personal and societal contradictions. We owe it to Ms. Jacobs. We owe it to the ancestors.

ACKNOWLEDGMENTS

Thank you first and foremost to Harriet Jacobs; your courage, intelligence, sensitivity, and persistence have left us with a lasting legacy and a reason to strive always to be humble, serving, grateful, and better than we are. Now I shall run through a list of names of people and institutions who have made such an indelible and positive impact on this work: Emilya Cachapero, NEA/TCG Theatre Residency Program for Playwrights, Martha Lavey, Hallie Gordon, Jocelyn Prince, Ed Sobel, Steppenwolf Theatre Ensemble, Dr. Don Quinn Kelley, Derek Walcott, Kate Snoddgrass, Megan Sandberg-Zakian, Jean Fagan Yellin, Debra Wise, Underground Railway Theatre, Ilana Brownstein, Nambi E. Kelley, Eric Rosen, Jessica Thebus, Rebecca Stevens, Kansas City Rep, Russ Tutterow, Marsha Estell, Chicago Dramatists, Arena Stage, Duke University, and all of the actors who have so courageously given their considerable talents, intellects, and hearts to this project. Finally, thank you John and Baylor for giving me the reason to do what I do, and the support to keep doing it. I love you. And Mommy, thank you, because I never get to put that in writing, and you made me, and nurtured me, and will enjoy highlighting this sentence and showing it to your friends, who, in turn, may buy the book.

PRODUCTION HISTORY

Harriet Jacobs was commissioned and the world premiere produced by Steppenwolf Theatre Company (Martha Lavey, artistic director; David Hawkanson, executive director) as a part of its Steppenwolf for Young Adults programming. The production ran from February 8 to March 2, 2008, with the following cast:

Harriet Jacobs	Nambi E. Kelley
Grandma/Ensemble	Celeste Williams
Master Norcom/Ensemble	Kenn E. Head
Mary/Mistress Norcom/Ensemble	Leslie Ann Sheppard
Tom/Ensemble	Christoph Horton Abiel
Samuel Treadwell Sawyer/Ensemble	Sean Walton
Ensemble	Genevieve VenJohnson
Ensemble	Errón Jay

Director	Hallie Gordon
Scenic Design	Collette Pollard
Lighting Design	J. R. Lederle
Costume Design	Ana Kuzmanic
Sound Design	Victoria DeIorio
Choreographer	Lisa Johnson-Willingham
Composer	McKinley Johnson
Dramaturge	Jocelyn Prince
Stage Manager	Calyn P. Swain
Assistant Stage Manager	Kim Forbes

Harriet Jacobs was subsequently produced by Underground Railway Theater (Debra Wise, artistic director) at Central Square Theater (Catherine Carr Kelly, executive director) and ran from January 7 to January 31, 2010, with the following cast:

Harriet Jacobs . . . . Kami Rushell Smith
Grandma/Ensemble . . . . Ramona Lisa Alexander
Mary/Ensemble . . . . Obehi Janice
Tom/Ensemble . . . . Sheldon Best
Harold/Ensemble . . . . Mishell Lilly
Mistress Norcom/Ensemble . . . . Kortney Adams
Master Norcom/Ensemble . . . . Raidge
Samuel Treadwell Sawyer/Ensemble . . . . De'Lon Grant

Director . . . . Megan Sandberg-Zakian
Scenic and Object Design . . . . Susan Zeeman Rogers
Costume Design . . . . Charles Schoonmaker
Lighting Design . . . . David Roy
Musical Director/Composer . . . . Dr. Clarice LaVerne Thompson
Choreographer . . . . Melody Ruffin Ward
Assistant Director . . . . Denise Washington
Stage Manager . . . . Dominique D. Burford
Assistant Stage Manager . . . . Christine D. White

Harriet Jacobs was subsequently produced by Kansas City Repertory Theatre (Eric Rosen, artistic director; Jerry Genochio, producing director; Cynthia Rider, managing director) and ran from October 22 to November 21, 2010, with the following cast:

Harriet Jacobs . . . . Nambi E. Kelley
Grandma . . . . Cheryl Lynn Bruce
Tom/Ensemble . . . . Phillip James Brannon
Master Norcom/Ensemble . . . . David Fonteno
Mary/Ensemble . . . . Shamika Cotton
Mistress Norcom/Ensemble . . . . Ronica Reddick
Samuel Treadwell Sawyer/Ensemble . . . . Gilbert Glenn Brown
Daniel/Ensemble . . . . Damron Russel Armstrong

Director . . . . Jessica Thebus
Scenic Design . . . . Collette Pollard

Costume Design . . . . Jeremy W. Floyd

Lighting Design . . . . J. R. Lederle

Production Design . . . . Jeffrey Cady

Composer/Sound Design . . . . Andre Pluess

Movement Director . . . . Tyrone Aiken

Assistant Director . . . . Rebecca Stevens

Casting Director, New York . . . . Stephanie Klapper

Chicago Casting . . . . Cree Rankin

Stage Manager . . . . Mary R. Honour

HARRIET JACOBS

CHARACTERS

Note: It is imperative that all cast members are Black. All "White" characters are represented by Black ensemble members, donning skeletal white hoopskirts, bonnets, top hats, and the like. It is important that some theatrical gesture (for example, putting on gloves or white skirts onstage) accompany the transforming of ensemble members into "White" characters.

Harriet Jacobs — Age fourteen to nineteen. The author of one of the first published slave narratives, Harriet possesses an intelligence and centeredness beyond her years. These traits are equally attributable to the strength that surely any slave must have had to possess and a personal wisdom and acuity passed down from insightful parents and grandparents. Harriet has a social savvy—a dexterity that serves her well both with her family or peers and with slave owners. She's very educated and slips easily between the more casual slave vernacular of the time and the formal language used in her writing and when addressing the audience. She is not "putting this on" or "talking proper"; she is an adept and unconscious "code-switcher." Historically, Harriet is described as having light-brown skin and dark eyes. She is the daughter of two Biracial parents. She is pretty but does not embrace or consciously exploit her looks; in her setting they are more often a liability than a blessing, and she is aware of this.

Grandma	Harriet's strong-willed, well-liked, free grandmother.
Mary	African American, fifteen. In awe and dangerously jealous of Harriet. A house servant and field hand with fewer of Harriet's social and linguistic graces.
Tom	African American, eighteen. Handsome, strong, good-natured, charismatic. He loves Harriet. Tom is a carpenter and a slave on a neighboring plantation.
Master Norcom	The "White" master, fifty to sixty-five. The town doctor, he carries himself with a confident swagger. He fancies himself a godly, family man. (Avoid casting him as the obvious villain.)
Mistress Norcom	The "White" mistress, twenty-seven. A faded flower. Once beautiful and carefree, she is now a victim of her environment. She is hateful toward her female slaves and wary of her husband. She has borne a child a year since her marriage at seventeen.
Samuel Treadwell Sawyer	"White" lawyer in his thirties. From a prestigious family. He is intrigued by Harriet's intellect and physically attracted to her. He is probably not "in love" with her.
Harold	Slave. Various ensemble roles. Played by the same actor as Master Norcom.
Charlotte	Slave. Various ensemble roles. Played by the same actress as Mistress Norcom.
Daniel	A field slave. Various other ensemble roles.

Joshua	A field slave. Various other ensemble roles. Played by the same actor as Samuel Treadwell Sawyer.
Isaac	Slave. Various ensemble roles. Played by the same actor as Tom.
"White" Lady 1 and 2	Patrons of Grandma's bakery. Played by the actresses who play Mary and Charlotte, respectively.
Joseph (optional)	Harriet's son, seven. The children are not necessarily required to speak, given that their speaking parts are heard from offstage. Where the children are visible, their roles may also be played by other ensemble members, or the director may decide to not have them visible at all, in which case some scenes as written here would need to be adjusted. (Earlier productions did not cast actual children for the roles. Should a production choose to, it is probably better if they still not speak. Ensemble members can speak their offstage lines.)
Louisa (optional)	Harriet's daughter, six.

ACT 1

SCENE 1

[*A light reveals a crude wooden shed, about eight feet high. The shed has only the suggestion of walls and a roughly hewn, slanted roof—it is only slightly larger than the space under a conference-room table.*]

[*Two male cast members unlatch the sides of the structure's roof to reveal* HARRIET *lying on her stomach, writing by candlelight in the small space, now indicated by a skeletal frame.*]

[*The candle goes out. Blackness.*]

HARRIET: It is a dark that is darker than light. [HARRIET *strikes a match, lights a candle, and writes furiously. The candle blows out. Darkness.*] Blacker even than that. [HARRIET *lights the candle again, resumes writing. After a moment she notices the audience.*] Today, black and small and damp and cold. Tomorrow, maybe hot and dry. Full of splinters that bite, and mites that bite, and vermin that bite. Are you there? I am never sure. I see faces in my darkness . . . until I am alone, again.

[HARRIET *climbs down the ladder and crosses to the center.*]

I must explain. [HARRIET *rolls up her sleeves.*] If you would understand. Please. I try to understand myself. This reality that has brought me to this reality. I try to make sense of it, and so I ask that you try as well. I fear that if I say to you that what I experienced under the cruel hand of slavery was unspeakable . . . I fear that you would incline your heads a bit to the left or the right and say, "Yes, I understand, poor girl," and think no more of it. I fear more that you might throw your head back in exasperation and say, "Tell us something we have not already heard." I promise, I shall try. We shall all try. [*Music begins, low, under* HARRIET'*s words.*] I promise that you may believe you have heard it, you may believe you know this, and I suggest that it is slightly beyond knowing, because still, I hear the stories, I live the stories, and I do not yet understand. [*Beat.*] This is the flesh. My flesh. My feet. My head. My heart. It is all I have to offer. It is all we have to offer.

[*Male* ENSEMBLE *members emerge from the shadows, transforming the austere stage into Grandmother's kitchen.*]

I have misspoken. Not ours. Not *my* flesh. Not *my* body. Even now, not mine. [*Touching her body, beat.*] *My* soul. This is mine. This has always been mine. My heart, my soul, this is what I wish to share. With you.

[*Light rises on an old lady kneading bread on a small table by a hearth: Harriet's* GRANDMA.]

GRANDMA: Who are you talking to?

HARRIET: To *whom* am I talking Grandma . . .

GRANDMA: I am sure my granddaughter is not tellin' *me* how to speak . . .

HARRIET: I'm jes' teasing with you.

GRANDMA [*laughing*]: Better be . . . 'cause seems to me, I'm the one taught you, in your diapers, to say your first words . . . so, who were you talkin' to . . . ?

HARRIET: Oh, I was just . . . just thinking.

GRANDMA: Well stop that. Life *is*. We pray to the Lord for deliverance, love the people before us whom we must love, wipe our butts, roll up our sleeves, and work. No time for thinking.

HARRIET [*laughing*]: Wipe our butts? What's gotten into you?

GRANDMA: Little bit of the devil today I s'pose. Did I add the leavening?

HARRIET: Probably.

GRANDMA: Take that batch out, they smell ready.

[HARRIET *moves to look out of the window.*]

HARRIET: It's getting late . . .

GRANDMA: They burning . . .

HARRIET [*removing the crackers from the oven*]: She'll have my hide.

GRANDMA: So take the mistress a package of warm crackers. Tell her Grandmother wouldn't let you leave 'fore they come out. How many babies she drop, one a year fo de lass six years? Tell her maybe if she cross her legs and eat a cracker, wouldn't be in that condition all the time.

[HARRIET'*s removing crackers from a cookie sheet as they speak.*]

HARRIET: If it's just the same to you, I think I won't tell her the latter.

GRANDMA: The latter? You need to watch it with the fancy talk.

HARRIET: I speak from my heart, and so, if my heart is smarter than my master's I cannot help it, and I will not apologize for it.

GRANDMA: Just tell me this. How he have time to run after skirt like he do . . . ? Got her always in the family way, seem he gettin' enough where he lay.

HARRIET: Grandmother stop . . .

GRANDMA: That's why she so mean, can't lay down for rest 'fore he tryin' to climb on top of her . . .

HARRIET: Grandmother . . .

GRANDMA: And if she do lay down, cain't rest proper tryin' to figure out who else he climbin' on top of. Should jes' be grateful for a moment of peace on her back . . . [*Both laugh.*]

[*The door opens, and two* "WHITE" LADIES *enter.* GRANDMA's *and* HARRIET's *postures change to proud deference—no hint of the mirth from the moment before.*]

"WHITE" LADY 1: Molly, I need corn bread for a stuffing . . .

GRANDMA [*pointedly*]: *Good evening* to you, ma'am.

"WHITE" LADY 1: Yes, of course . . . Good evening. [*Before* GRANDMA *can respond*] I need corn bread, the older and harder the better . . .

GRANDMA: Well ma'am, I jes' gave the pigs the day-olds, but if you slice the new down the middle and toast it, it should serve your dressing just fine.

"WHITE" LADY 2: I hope you have a pass Harriet.

GRANDMA: May I offer your order as a gift, an' in exchange you drop Harriet off at the back of the Norcom estate, splainin' to the mistress how you ran 'cross her here and asked her to help carry your load.

"WHITE" LADY 1: Then you will need to add a dozen vanilla wafers to the order.

GRANDMA: Yes ma'am.

"WHITE" LADY 1: And a couple of those petit fours.

GRANDMA: Yes ma'am.

"WHITE" LADY 2: Oh, well, I'll have a dozen wafers as well.

GRANDMA: Certainly. [*Beat.*] That'll be twelve cents.

"WHITE" LADY 2: Oh . . . [*She turns to* "WHITE" LADY 1, *who shrugs.*] Oh . . . [*She looks in her purse.*] Maybe just a half dozen then. [*She pays.*]

GRANDMA: Harriet, get your shawl.

HARRIET: Thank you Grandmother. I see you soon, I hope.

GRANDMA: I love you, baby. [*Pulling her aside*] Please try not to let that mouth get you in trouble.

SCENE 2

[HARRIET *enters, carrying a heavy bucket of water and ladle on her head. A rhythmic, muffled work song is heard under the scene.* HARRIET *sets down the bucket, removes a small book from her pocket, and begins to read.* TOM *walks up to her.* HARRIET *is startled and quickly puts the book in her pocket.*]

HARRIET: Lord! Tom! You near scared the devil out of me . . .

TOM: Harriet?

HARRIET: What you doin'?

TOM: Came to see you. I see what you doin'. You need to be more careful.

HARRIET: Had a moment, thought the workers could use a bit of water. An' they wasn't here, an' I was at a real good place in the story . . . [*Beat. They stand and grin at one another.*] Tom.

TOM: Uh huh . . .

HARRIET: Naw, I ain't got nothin' to say, I jes' like the way it sounds . . . Tom. I like the way it taste, your name in my mouth.

TOM: Seems like the name Ezekiel or Elijah might taste better in your mouth.

HARRIET: Maybe would, but I fancy Tom. [*Beat. Teasing*] If you think it best, I might could go lookin' for a 'Zekiel or a 'Lijah to spend my time with.

TOM: Brought somethin' to show you.

[TOM *pulls an ornate piece of a banister out of his bag.*]

HARRIET: It's beautiful. [*Beat.*] What is it?

TOM: It's the part what holds up a banister. See how sturdy but handsome to look at? I made a tool that makes it easy to do with just one piece of wood. It's a trick in it, an' I figured out how, an' I think it's gone set me up real nice. In jes' a few minutes all Master's cronies gone be asking to hire me out to give them somethin' so fancy.

HARRIET: It's clever. You think you get your own shop one day?

TOM: May, or may be I jes' be a carpenter for hire. Make a living, support a family someday.

[HARRIET *smiles shyly but doesn't allow the tone to change to be as serious as* TOM *would have it.*]

HARRIET [*putting her hands behind her back*]: Guess which one . . .

TOM: I don' have time for playin' games . . .

HARRIET: Jes' guess.

[TOM *points to a hand.* HARRIET *opens it, and a ball of cotton falls out.*]

Good. Try again.

[HARRIET *picks up the cotton, puts her hands behind her back, and presents her fists again.*]

Twice. You get three right, I give you a kiss.

TOM: You silly.

[*And again she puts her fists out.*]

HARRIET: Awright then.

[TOM *guesses right a third time.* HARRIET *kisses him, quickly on the mouth.* TOM *starts to leave.*]

Wait Tom. Can you keep this for me, so we can play next time I see you, even if it's not in the cotton field. [TOM *crosses back.* HARRIET *hands him a cotton ball.*] Wait.

[*And the other from the other fist. They both laugh heartily.*]

TOM: You bad.

HARRIET: Yes I am. I most certainly am dear Tom.

[*As* TOM *exits, the work song becomes stronger until* HARRIET *is surrounded by workers. The work is shown in synchronized, highly choreographed, rhythmic movement. Eventually, each worker drops his or her song to sip from the kettle and sit under a tree. When the last worker has taken a sip and the bucket with him, the song has finally dwindled.*]

[*To audience*] If you have not seen a cotton field, when the cotton is almost ready for picking, you have missed one of the most beautiful sights God has given us. I like to kneel in the middle of an open field so the cotton is just below my eyes. For as far as you can see it looks like a soft blanket or maybe even heaven. I think God has given the South cotton because he does not often give us snow.

[*Song begins, continues under.*]

Sometimes I lie on my back and look at the clouds, and I feel as though I just might melt on up into them. I close my eyes an' try not to think . . .

HAROLD: Name's Harold. Work de fields. Forty-sebben years ol'. Live here all my life. Blessed by God 'cause I never got solt away from my fambly.

HARRIET: . . . I am sorry for you if you have not seen a cotton field, when the cotton is almost ready for picking.

HAROLD: Only time I remember a real beatin', was day 'fore my eighteenth birfday.

HARRIET: Is so soff . . .

HAROLD: Took a liken' to a young girl worked next ta me in de fields.

HARRIET: Juss soff an' white an' little specks of brown . . .

12

HAROLD: Overseer caught us spendin' time together 'hind a tree on break. She was a good girl.

HARRIET: It truly is breathtaking. It is the one time when I feel most unburdened.

HAROLD: Weren't doin' nothing put her in a way bring shame to her or her fambly.

HARRIET: . . . As though my heart would float up an' be one with the blue sky above me, and my body would just follow along.

HAROLD: So, dis overseer calls all de workers over . . .

HARRIET: Like I be light as a feather, maybe shifting this way and that, depending on the strength of the wind.

HAROLD: Make them stand all around us in a circle . . .

HARRIET: I close my eyes an' try to close my ears an' heart to the stories . . .

[HARRIET *lies down.*]

HAROLD: Overseer make us get undress an' tell us to do things we wouldna even done by ourselves.

HARRIET: The clouds real pretty . . .

HAROLD: Her mama, two aunts, an' a grandpappy had to watch me lay on top of her. An' jes' then I think, don' matter what happen to me, 'cause de Lord don' wan' people ackin' like dis.

HARRIET: And the blue of the sky bluer than any blue . . .

HAROLD: An' I get offa her an' ah put on my pants, an' ah tell Overseer he gone have to finish what I start 'cause I too young to go ta hell fo his sins. An' he beat me so hard I couldn't lay down t'sleep fo the pain. Only part my body not scarred to dis day from dat beatin's de bottom my feet.

HARRIET: Maybe the sky not that blue . . .

HAROLD: De girl, don't know what had happen' to her.

[*Silence. A shift.*]

HARRIET: I see the blood and sweat and tears dripping off my pretty cotton, and it not so pretty. [*Beat.*] My work is elsewhere. Easier because I do it with a roof over my head, shoes on my feet, and the North Carolina sun off my back. [HARRIET *steps downstage and speaks to the audience so the field slaves can't hear.*] Harder maybe 'cause I see life on the other side of misery. Harder 'cause I live under the feet of the Whites who wish us to believe that we are animals.

[*The light shifts to indicate a move inside of the house. Bags that had been slung over arms for picking and bundles that represented babies on backs reveal a small chandelier, candles, aprons the women don, vests the men put on, furniture, and so on. It is all hustle and bustle as the field hands become house servants.*]

It is quite amazing, really, the inner workings of the "big house." [*Rhythmic work music begins.*] I don't think Mistress Norcom would know how to keep it going were it not for the administrative skills of the head male servant, the female cook, and the various household talents of the rest of us.

[*The "house" is set up as* HARRIET *speaks. This is both a highly choreographed depiction of* HARRIET'S *workday and a portrayal of the cat-and-mouse game that goes on between* HARRIET *and the* MASTER. *The whole* ENSEMBLE *is involved.*]

First thing in the morning, before the sun comes up, I empty the bedpans. [MASTER NORCOM *hands* HARRIET *a bedpan, catches her wrist, and whispers into her ear.*] I then rekindle the fires in each and every room. I help the mistress with her morning toilette . . . [*A servant transforms into the mistress with* HARRIET's *assistance as she talks.* MASTER NORCOM *lurks but does not approach* HARRIET.] This includes the second removal of a bedpan, heating and carrying water for a bath, the combing and arranging of hair, stockings, petticoats, and skirts, and the fastening of each and every button. [*As* HARRIET *leaves the* MISTRESS, MASTER NORCOM *catches the* MISTRESS *by her wrist, whispers in her ear, and pats her bottom. She exits.* MASTER NORCOM *walks to* HARRIET *and whispers in her ear.*] Once the house is awake, I hang the rugs on the line out back and beat them. I wash and polish the floors. [MASTER NORCOM *admires her in her knelt position.*] I clear and wash breakfast dishes. I dust each baseboard. I wash the windows. I polish the silver. [MASTER NORCOM *whispers in her ear.*] I clear and wash the lunch dishes. I mend clothes, darn socks, and iron linens. I lay the rugs back down. [MASTER NORCOM *whispers.*] And on and on it goes. And this is my reality. But worse than mine, today . . . are the stories that never stop . . .

[*The hustle and bustle and the rhythms and movement of work continue at top speed. A very old* CHARLOTTE *steps forward, struggling with a basket of laundry. The work continues behind her.*]

CHARLOTTE: I born here. People 'member de ol' master an' missus as decent an' good 'cause dey went to church, hab a big, well-dressed fambly, an' kep' all us slaves clean an' fed. Dat massa, de doctor's daddy, was always after me, had me too, 'cause I was der and dat's what dey could do. Missus din' like it. She always steady lookin' at me like I her worsest en'my. Affer my third baby come out lookin' mo like de massa din de massa hisself, she come to my cabin, night affer de birf, an' takes him. Don' know if she kilt de baby or solt him. I think prob'ly kilt him 'cause none de house servants never could look me in de eyes affer dat. Still, dey kep' me on, an' one day she jes' start ta beatin' me wiff a iron kettle rod. She sho woulda beat me to my deaf, loss my leff eye dat day, but de rod broke an' she had to stop long 'nuff to hear me say, "God fo sho cryin' fo you today." I say, "I sho wouldn't treat a dog as you treatin' me." An' she stop an' commence to fall on de flo' cryin', an' I comfort her. Later I get a whippin' 'cause some blood dripped on the mistress's silk skirts. Dey long dead now.

[CHARLOTTE *recedes into the working* ENSEMBLE. *Their efforts dwindle, and they exit as* HARRIET *steps forward.*]

HARRIET: The only real escape is the time I spend in the loving cocoon of Grandmother's kitchen with the two people I love most in the world. It is not just the sweet smell of cinnamon rolls mingled with the sharp scents of sage and parsley . . . it is the warm embrace of unconditional love. The comfort of my steady Tom and Grandma's incomparable sass . . .

[*As* HARRIET *speaks, she moves into Grandma's kitchen where* GRANDMA *and* TOM *sit, eating biscuits and gravy.*]

GRANDMA: "Incomparable sass" . . . there you go again with the words.

TOM: We love your words Harriet . . . But I still tryin' to see whatchu gettin' at?

HARRIET: Jes' that I believe there are two kinds of mean mistresses.

TOM: It don't matter.

HARRIET: Hear me Tom . . . There are mistresses who know that this . . .

GRANDMA: What?

HARRIET: How it is . . . this way we live . . . Slavery . . .

GRANDMA: Lord have mercy . . . can't you never talk 'bout who was seen goin' into the toolshed with who . . . like a normal girl. An' I don't like to gossip, but it was Annie an' that boy what works in the house, they call him Red . . .

HARRIET: Still, I am making a point. There are those mistresses who know that this thing, this way we live, slavery, is evil and wrong and so lash out because they must convince themselves that we are animals that they might sleep at night and hold their heads up in church on Sunday morning.

GRANDMA [*offering* TOM *another biscuit*]: Another biscuit Tom?

TOM: Please. Thank you ma'am.

GRANDMA: I jes' noticed 'cause I think Red at least five years younger than that girl. An' whatever they was doin' in the toolshed, they didn't come out the shed with not even a hammer . . .

HARRIET: It is as though I am not talking.

TOM: It is never as though you are not talking.

HARRIET: And then there are those mistresses who would treat their own meanly and so certainly would have no regard for us. An' all of them, steady gettin' treated mean by they own men.

TOM: And God sees only the mean behavior and would not care why.

HARRIET: If I can distinguish between the two, certainly God can.

GRANDMA: Because you sit on the right hand of God the Father Almighty?

HARRIET: Because I have the thought, and the thought must be put there by God.

TOM: Now you sound like the master. "God has told me that I must take care of you black heathens because you cannot see after yourselves."

HARRIET: I just think that the mistress who only beats me because she is miserable, hurts when she does, and so will be judged accordingly.

GRANDMA: And so you believe you'll sit at the table of milk and honey next to the woman who beat you?

HARRIET: Oh no Granny, she'll be servin' me at the table.

TOM [*laughing*]: See this is what brings me round even when I may pay for it tomorrow.

GRANDMA: I thought it was my biscuits.

TOM: You thought wrong old lady.

HARRIET: Tom!

GRANDMA [*laughing*]: He's right, start thinkin' too much of yourself when folks all time tellin' you 'bout your talents.

TOM: Those talents bought your freedom, so you keep right on thinkin' highly of them.

GRANDMA: But long as he owns my kin, I am still under the thumb of the good Doctor Norcom.

HARRIET: He can't touch you—he wouldn't dare. Don't want the town to see his true colors.

TOM: Truth be told, it is your beauty, not your biscuits, brings me round.

HARRIET: What about my beauty?

GRANDMA: Don' worry, I ain' gone steal yo man.

TOM: I think you should worry, Harriet. Grandma lookin' good today . . .

GRANDMA: I'm goin' to the shed, be back in four minutes.

[GRANDMA *exits to shed.* HARRIET *moves to* TOM's *lap.*]

TOM: You noticed she always tellin' us jes' how long. "I be back in three an' a half minutes, an' forty seconds."

HARRIET: But it's never long enough for me to get a good kiss.

[*They kiss.*]

TOM: I thought that was pretty good.

HARRIET: But not long enough.

[*They kiss again.*]

TOM: Long enough for me to get worked up though.

HARRIET: She wants you worked up, so you'll ask for my hand.

TOM: I woulda done that a long time ago if I thought it was yours to give.

HARRIET: So you would deprive me the joy of hearing you ask?

TOM: To spare myself the pain of having him say no. Or worse, he convince my master to sell me away.

HARRIET: Or sell me away.

TOM: He ain't thinkin' 'bout sellin' you away. Not how he be all the time lookin' at you.

HARRIET: Doesn't that bother you?

TOM: I lose my mind, I be bothered by that. He is still just lookin' at you?

HARRIET: Yes, but don't say nothin' to Grandma 'bout it, please. She worry too much, may even say somethin' cross to him and get me sold down the river. [*Beat.*] Tom, you think we can run from this one day?

TOM: We ain' gone have to run. We gone buy our freedom.

HARRIET: Don' you think we gone make some pretty, smart babies Tom?

TOM: Don' know I wan' bring babies into dis kind of a world.

HARRIET: Don' think there's nothin' you can do 'bout that. Not if you love me like you says you do. 'Sides, ain' gone make no babies jes' kissen' fo four minutes . . .

TOM: I can wait Harriet . . . we say the words, jump de broom, and *then* make the babies . . . We ain't got to live like animals, jes' 'cause we got to live like animals.

GRANDMA: Here I come . . . into the kitchen . . .

HARRIET: Here she come into the kitchen . . .

GRANDMA: Hope I don't see nothin' an old woman ain't s'posed to see . . .

HARRIET [*jumping off of* TOM's *lap*]: What you not s'posed to see Grandma? Tell me, so I'll be sure not to be doin' it next time you go to the shed for four minutes.

GRANDMA: Tom, hadn't you better be goin' now? Gettin' close to sundown.

TOM: Yes'm. Can I just have one kiss to hold me in the fields next week?

GRANDMA: 'Course you can.

[TOM *looks as though he's walking to* HARRIET *for a last embrace, steps past her, and sweeps* GRANDMA *into a dip, kissing her loudly on the cheek.*]

TOM: Be seein' you ladies.

GRANDMA: You be careful de paddy rollers don't getchu. [TOM *exits. To* HARRIET] He a mess.

HARRIET: 'Bout the prettiest, nicest, most hardworking mess this side the Mississippi, an' he chose me.

GRANDMA: I'm glad to see you lettin' your heart go for a change.

HARRIET: I didn't let it go; he jes' grabt a hold of it faster'n I could keep it. You know the master won't let us.

GRANDMA: Yes. But you got to let Tom be a man and try.

[TOM *pokes his head back in the door.*]

TOM: Almost forgot. Grandma, it all right wit' you if I ask Harriet for her hand?

GRANDMA: Whatchu think Tom?

TOM: How 'bout Harriet, you give me your blessing to go to Master Norcom and ask for your hand?

[HARRIET *runs and hugs him.*]

HARRIET: You have my blessing! Always did . . . now go, 'fo your overseer make it so you cain't come back.

[TOM *exits. Light rises on* DANIEL.]

DANIEL: I's always big, like my daddy, and 'cause of it d'overseer use me ta do his wuppin'. He say, "Daniel commere," an' han' me de whip and yell me to keep goin' 'til he say stop. Las' week I kilt Sam an' Nancy's girl, couldna been mo den twelve. Didn' mean to. He jes' keep sayin', "Give her 'nother," an' I has to do it. I don' wan' do it. I has to. Or it be me get beat. I cain't get a wife, cain't have no friends 'cause of it. Truly, I ain't a bad person. Truly I ain't.

SCENE 3

[HARRIET *and* MARY *scrub the floor and talk.*]

HARRIET: And they was so pretty . . . I gone have a little girl some day. It jes' . . . it made me sad Mary.

MARY: I don't see whas so sad 'bout that.

HARRIET: It's the way little girls play together.

MARY: And . . .

HARRIET: And it broke my heart.

MARY: Hand me the rinse pail. Way I see it, your heart break too easy. You ain't gone live to see twenty-five.

HARRIET: Why I wanna live to be an old lady anyway?

[*The very pregnant* MISTRESS NORCOM *enters stage left and walks past.* HARRIET *and* MARY *scrub, never speaking, not taking their eyes off of her until she exits.*]

MARY: I jes' tellin' you. Your heart's too soff.

HARRIET: People always wanna confuse a soft heart for a soft soul. I'm jes' fine, thank you.

MARY: You welcome. You see Tom lately?

HARRIET: Why you ask?

MARY: You get tired of him, you let me know . . . I could make him very happy.

HARRIET: You a mess. See, this what I mean. These girls, what I seen in the field, was playin' like they do before they get like us, an' let a man make them jealous. They ain't thinkin' 'bout how pretty they look or tryin' to impress a boy. They jes' lovin' each other and the day and the moment.

MARY: Whas this?

[MARY *points to a spot on the floor.* HARRIET *leans over and scrapes the mark with her thumbnail.*]

HARRIET: Thas from those new shoes Mistress got from Paris. They paint the soles black.

MARY: Well them fashionable shoes gonna get us a whippin' fo sho.

[*Both girls stop their talking and scrub furiously. It's a frantic, frightened scrubbing. Finally, the spot is removed. Both are relieved.*]

HARRIET: It was a little White girl and a little slave girl.

MARY: What?

HARRIET: What I was sayin' . . .

MARY: Das right . . .

HARRIET: You know I don't put much stock into yellow hair and blue eyes, but this lil girl cute, all pink cheeks and dimples and curls. And the other's the kind of pretty I wouldn't wish on no slave girl. She be lucky she keep her virtue 'til she twelve bein' that pretty. Red-brown, long, curly braids, and dimples too. Prob'ly they sisters. But I know they only got 'bout two mo years to love each other an' be friends, 'fo they know the truth.

MARY: It prob'ly only be bad fo the niggra gal.

HARRIET: 'Course it worse for her, but the other one gone lose her best friend the day she know she own her best friend. And then, maybe five years later, they both look each other in the face real good and know the truth 'bout who they daddy is. An' it won't make no difference.

MARY: 'Cept prob'ly the mistress sell her long 'fore that.

HARRIET: You ain't said a word. Don't wish pretty on no one.

MARY: You pretty, an' I ain't half-bad myself.

HARRIET: That's why we in de big house, but you know there's some prettier an' smarter'n us. Heard 'bout that girl down on the Simms place? Took a flatiron to her own face ta keep de massa an' his sons away from her.

MARY: I told you 'bout that.

HARRIET: I'll get the fresh water.

MARY: Thas all right. I finished here. I'll put back the furniture and do the entryway if you bleach and boil the diapers.

HARRIET: That lye bleach eat the skin off my fingers.

MARY: Poor Harriet. Maybe try fo'teen hours picken' an' shuckin' corn an' talk to me 'bout your hands.

HARRIET: I sorry Mary. I forget you got ta work outside too.

MARY: Don't pity me, jes' don' be complainin' 'bout a little lye bleach.

[HARRIET *finds a spot downstage right, as the light fades on* MARY *furiously drying the floor.*]

[HARRIET *takes diapers off of a line and puts them in a large bucket, poking occasionally at them with a large stick. She sits on an upside-down pail and pulls a small novel from under her apron.*]

HARRIET: "... Under the trees whose boughs made a friendly darkness, the amorous D'Elmont throwing his eager arms round the virtuous Melliora's waist, placed burning kisses upon her neck, [*male* ENSEMBLE *begins reciting the same words*] creating in her, a kind of ecstasy, [*female* ENSEMBLE *begins reciting the passage at "Under the trees ..."*] which might perhaps, had they been now alone, proved her desires were little different from his ..."

[ENSEMBLE *voices have layered in, turning the passage into a round of sorts; it can go on for a while, finally fading out as* HARRIET *speaks.*]

Lost in the pages of a book, I travel into exciting lands and become princesses and fair maidens. They always *fair,* but in my mind they look jes' like me. In books, I am beautiful and virtuous, well dressed, and always rescued by a handsome man who loves me for my beauty and my innate kindness. Innate kindness. I like the way that sounds. [HARRIET *closes the book.*] When I learned to read, it was my mistress before this one who taught me. The master's now-dead sister. I do not think she taught me because she was particularly "virtuous" or, "innately kind." I think she taught me because she was bored, as any sane woman resigned to a life of childbirth and frivolity would be. I also think she was not at all bright and did not consider that once she taught me to read, I would then and forevermore know how to read. It was as though my acquiring of each letter, each syllable, each phonetic advancement was an amusing miracle ... but it had not occurred to her that those things might stay in my mind. Mistress Norcom would know better ...

[MISTRESS NORCOM *has approached* HARRIET *from behind.*]

You startled me ma'am.

MISTRESS NORCOM: What are you doing?

HARRIET [*still holding the book*]: Bleaching the diapers.

MISTRESS NORCOM: Hand me that.

[HARRIET *"innocently" offers the bucket of diapers.* MISTRESS NORCOM *slaps her and gestures to the book.*]

Not only does she read, an act punishable by death, but she reads garbage. What will the good doctor do when I tell him?

[HARRIET *assumes an exaggerated "slave" dialect.*]

HARRIET: I'z sorry. Pleeeze may ah go back to mah work?

MISTRESS NORCOM: Perhaps he'll finally give you the flogging you deserve and send you to the auction block.

HARRIET: It true, the Hacketts comin' by at noon? I really oughta make haste and lays out de table [*beat*] so's it bees ready for dem.

MISTRESS NORCOM: You seein' that Black field nigga from the Stewart plantation?

HARRIET: Don't know whatchu mean ma'am?

MISTRESS NORCOM: Stop acting dumb and answer me plain. Have you been spending time with that Black boy from the Stewarts' place?

HARRIET: Most de slaves on de Stewarts' plantation Black.

MISTRESS NORCOM: Jes' know that the blackest one came shufflin' up to the back of the house this mornin' asking for an audience with the master. The doctor and I were just getting settled at the breakfast table. I answer the door and says, "And what is this regarding?"

[*In another area of the stage,* MASTER NORCOM *and* TOM *stand separately. Each becomes visible to the audience when an individual light illuminates him or becomes more intense as the actor speaks. The scenes overlap.*]

And he says,

TOM AND MISTRESS NORCOM: If it please you jes' as much,

TOM: I'd like to make my business wit' de massa hisself.

MISTRESS NORCOM: Says it just like that,

TOM [*groveling*]: Wit' de massa hisself.

MISTRESS NORCOM: Don't seem like the way a boy spend time with our Harriet would say it, but he takes off his hat, and lowers his head and says those insulting words to me just like that. "Wit' de massa hisself."

TOM: If it please the mistress, I would be most grateful if I may speak with the master alone.

MISTRESS NORCOM: Just like I am too stupid to smell the insult. As though he might as well say . . .

TOM: Cain't do my business with you, you ain't nothing but a foolish gal. You ain't no good for nothin' but warmin' the bed and havin' babies.

MISTRESS NORCOM: So I say, you wait just right here. [*The* MASTER'*s light comes on, and the* MISTRESS *steps into it.*] And I get the good doctor, and I stand behind his left shoulder, because, of course, now I want to know what business does this dirty niggra have that's too important for my female ears. And he pulls out a filthy envelope with at least seven hundred greasy dollar bills in it and says,

TOM AND MISTRESS NORCOM: If it please de massa . . .

MISTRESS NORCOM: He in love wit' a servant girl . . .

TOM: . . . and I know the askin' price be somewhere in de fambly of five hunded. But I know de servant been in dis here family a long time, so I'sweetened the deal wit' two mo hunded,

MISTRESS NORCOM AND TOM: and would de kind massa . . .

TOM: . . . see in his heart fo to let me buy her into freedom wit' de money I earned for my own freedom, so's I might marry her and live outside of sin 'til such a time as my own good massa see his way to let me buy my freedom.

[*Light fades on* TOM *and* MASTER NORCOM.]

MISTRESS NORCOM: First I think, how a field nigga get that kind of money . . . ?

HARRIET: He a carpenter. Hire himself out on his off time . . .

MISTRESS NORCOM: Shut up that mouth. And then I think, this is a good day. Truly a glorious day. I will have extra pocket change and be rid of lazy Harriet, all at once. And may I share what the good doctor does then?

[*Light rises again on* MASTER NORCOM.]

He counts each and every one of those dirty bills, twice. And he says,

MASTER NORCOM: Which property is it you're so in love with as to give up your own freedom?

TOM: Harriet sir.

MISTRESS NORCOM: And my husband walks into the kitchen, throws the money in the fire, and says,

MASTER NORCOM: I'll sell her to you for eight hundred and fifty and not a penny less,

MASTER AND MISTRESS NORCOM: on the day hell freezes over.

[*Lights out on* MASTER NORCOM *and* TOM.]

MISTRESS NORCOM: I only tell you this because you are like family to me. And so, if we are to put up with one another for the rest of eternity, let it be understood: I will tolerate no more insolence. I will not be reminded of the skills my dear stupid sister-in-law imparted to you before her unfortunate demise. And I will not have you skulking about with my husband. [*Pause.*] Understood?

HARRIET: Yes.

MISTRESS NORCOM: I did not hear you clearly. You said?

HARRIET: Yes *ma'am.*

MISTRESS NORCOM: Now please get the table laid and make sure the cook has prepared a lunch for eight. We mustn't appear unready for the Hacketts. Are you crying?

HARRIET: No ma'am.

MISTRESS NORCOM: I didn't think so.

[*Lights out. Up immediately on:*]

SCENE 4

[*A worker,* JOSHUA, *steps forward.* HARRIET *hears his story as she crosses into Grandma's kitchen.*]

JOSHUA: Name's Joshua. I don' git beat. Firs time massa tried ta lay hand on me, I grabbed his whip, looked him in de eyes an' say, "I's a crazy nigga. I'll work hard fo you, pick twice much as any dem. Work wit' out complainin'. Mate wit' anyone you wan' match me wit'. But chu hit me, I'll kill you an' anyone I can take to hell wit' me 'fore dey kill me firs." Been here fifteen yeahs, sired gone on eighteen youngins, most sold time dey was three, pick three times mo den de res, an' ain' never been lashed by none 'em. Don' s'pose I evah will.

[*Lights fade on* JOSHUA *and rise as* HARRIET *enters Grandma's kitchen.*]

HARRIET: It's been three weeks. He ain't comin' back is he?

GRANDMA: Is that my good morning?

HARRIET: Sorry. He ain't comin' back?

GRANDMA: How many times you gone ask?

HARRIET: Why I try make him marry me? We coulda gone on like we was . . . maybe do like others an' even make babies.

GRANDMA: You know I love Tom. But you still jes' a girl. An' if he cain't find the man in him to show his face, you the better for it. There's other men.

HARRIET: Maybe it is time for me to run . . .

GRANDMA: Hush. You run, get yourself killed, or, worse, [*beat*] I'll kill you myself. I got a hen lays when she feels like it . . . I think she'll fry up nice.

HARRIET: What I'm s'posed to do?

GRANDMA: Girl, you need to cry for five minutes and be about your business. Mind the shop for me for jes' a minute, got a hen to strangle. [GRANDMA *exits, reenters.*] And your five minutes was up 'bout ten days ago.

[GRANDMA *exits.* HARRIET *removes her work apron and wipes a countertop.* SAMUEL TREADWELL SAWYER, *a "White" gentleman, enters.*]

30

SAWYER: Good evening.

HARRIET: Yes sir.

SAWYER: Afternoon really.

HARRIET: Yes sir. [*Long pause.*] Is there something I may help you with?

SAWYER: That depends.

[*Long pause.*]

HARRIET: Yes sir?

SAWYER: Only if you will do me the honor of looking at me.

HARRIET: I don't understand.

SAWYER: I feel I am competing with your shoes. Are they very special?

HARRIET: My shoes?

SAWYER: Do you find your shoes more interesting than I?

HARRIET: I don't know. How interesting do you find my shoes?

SAWYER [*laughing*]: Do you find your shoes more interesting than I, *am*?

HARRIET: I don't know you. My shoes are safe. And predictable. And will not accuse me of impudence if I look at them.

SAWYER: I should like a half-dozen sourdough rolls, please.

HARRIET [*still not looking up*]: Yes sir.

SAWYER: What is your favorite?

HARRIET: It depends on the day.

SAWYER: The quality of the baked goods changes daily?

HARRIET: No sir. My preferences change daily.

SAWYER: My name is Samuel Treadwell Sawyer.

HARRIET: Yes sir.

SAWYER: Have you a name?

HARRIET: Yes sir. [*Beat.*] Just the rolls then?

SAWYER: Something sweet.

HARRIET: Grandmother makes a nice shortbread with just a touch of jam in the middle.

SAWYER: Then a dozen please.

[HARRIET *busies herself putting the baked goods in a basket. The gentleman is more and more intrigued.* HARRIET *has still not made eye contact.*]

Do you live here?

HARRIET: You must be new in town then?

SAWYER: Yes and no. My family has been here for some time, the Sawyer estate. I've recently returned from the North, where I practiced law. [*Beat.*] So, I ask again. Do you live here?

HARRIET: No sir. My grandmother is free and owns this house and business. I belong on the Norcom plantation, down the road.

SAWYER: Your grandmother is not here?

HARRIET: My grandmother will be here shortly.

SAWYER: You speak very well.

HARRIET: Thank you, so do you.

SAWYER: You seem sad . . .

[HARRIET *meets his gaze for the first time.*]

HARRIET: It shows?

SAWYER: Well then how much do I owe you?

[GRANDMA *enters, hand around the neck of the dead hen. She crosses quickly to examine the contents in the basket.*]

GRANDMA: Five cents for the rolls, ten for the shortbread. Five for the basket if you ain't bringin' it back.

HARRIET: And one for the lemon snickerdoodle.

SAWYER [*amused*]: Snickerdoodle . . . ?

HARRIET: My preference [*beat*] today.

SAWYER: Well thank you. And thank your grandmother for me.

GRANDMA: You may thank me yourself.

SAWYER: What is your granddaughter's name?

GRANDMA: She is fifteen . . .

SAWYER: I am only asking for future . . .

GRANDMA: She belongs to the Norcom plantation . . . [*Beat.*] Would there be anything else for you then?

SAWYER: No, thank you ma'am. I will bring back the basket. Pleasant day then.

[SAWYER *hands* HARRIET *the money;* GRANDMA *intercepts and pockets it. He exits.*]

HARRIET: He seems nice enough.

GRANDMA: A "nice" White man's more dangerous than a mean one.

HARRIET: Why?

GRANDMA: This is my experience. [*Pause.*] There are things I should have told you, about men and women . . .

HARRIET: I know about relations.

GRANDMA: You know?

HARRIET: I've heard.

GRANDMA: You must not leave yourself open to men who will degrade you. [*Beat.*] Has the master ever laid a hand on you?

HARRIET: No ma'am.

GRANDMA: Has he ever asked you for extra favors?

HARRIET: Grandma surely you know the master is bigger and stronger, and if he wants . . .

GRANDMA: I'm talking about the stupid girl who thinks her body a bargaining chip for an easier life. It's never the case. Because your body and soul are not valued by the men who ask for it.

HARRIET: You heard about Rose Cabarrison? Her young master fell in love with her and freed her and her children and her mammy too.

GRANDMA: And you think that's freedom?

HARRIET: A little house on the edge of town look like freedom to me.

GRANDMA: That little house ain't on the edge of town, that house on the edge of the Cabarrison plantation. 'Sides, it look like a slave cabin wit' a coat of white paint and flowers in the yard to me. You look inside that house, you'd see they not free.

HARRIET: I don't understand . . .

GRANDMA: I made myself a trade of baking, 'staid of making myself the trade. I can bake even now that I ain't so much to look at. I can bake and earn my own keep, never mind the whims of some man with a family to support and no legal reason to stay true.

HARRIET: I promise, I would never compromise myself.

GRANDMA: Thas all I ask. You stay ignorant to his advances, stay near the mistress and the kids. You be the good girl I have raised you to be.

HARRIET: Yes ma'am.

GRANDMA: 'Cept on your wedding night . . .

HARRIET: Grandma . . .

GRANDMA: Don't be a good girl on your wedding night. Wedding beds are made for fun. I bore your grandfather three healthy babies from a loving bed . . .

HARRIET: You had six children . . .

GRANDMA: I bore your grandfather three. [*Beat.*] You understand?

HARRIET: Yes ma'am.

GRANDMA: Good.

HARRIET: You really think I'll marry one day?

GRANDMA: Don't see why not. You young, you pretty, you can almost cook . . . and [*she thinks*] well, that's enough. You just need a good boy from the Norcom plantation, so's it don't require nothin' but a nod from the master. Put on a pot of grease so we can send some of this bird home with you 'fore dark.

[*Lights fade.*]

SCENE 5

[*Light rises on* MARY.]

MARY: Is jest the usual I guess. I work in de big house in de first of summer an' through de winter. Other times, I harvest de hay and de corn. Don' have ta pick cotton. Massa's brother came up to visit wit' his nephew. His nephew jes' turn thirteen. I fifteen. Massa an' his brother decide I what dey gone give de nephew fo his birfday. Not to have, jes' to use. I gone spare you de res.

[*Light fades on* MARY *and rises on* HARRIET.]

HARRIET [*to audience*]: Sometimes I wish he'd just force me like he do the others. But I'm special.

[*Light rises on* MASTER NORCOM, MARY, *and* MISTRESS NORCOM. *The following are three separate scenes that overlap in time and space.*]

MISTRESS NORCOM: You act like she's special James. She's just a slave girl.

MASTER NORCOM: You're special Harriet.

MARY: Ack like you think you so special.

HARRIET: I ain't listenin' to that Mary. [*To* MASTER NORCOM] You be needin' anything else this evening sir?

MASTER NORCOM: You know what I need.

HARRIET: I jes' be getting back to Miss Lizzie Mae and Junior then.

MASTER NORCOM: Why don' you come over here for a minute Harriet.

MISTRESS NORCOM: Harriet, I know the master put you in a new room at the end of the hall, but I want you to fix yourself up a pallet and sleep in the nursery with Lizzie Mae and Junior, cross the hall from me.

HARRIET: Massa, Lizzie Mae been having bad dreams lately, maybe you wan' me to go back to her, case she wake up distressed.

MASTER NORCOM: I want you to consider how sweet I could make your life.

HARRIET: My life all right now. [*Beat.*] Thank you.

MASTER NORCOM: Your hands are rough, dark circles under your eyes, your clothes always stained and dirty. Think how nice your life could be—if you lived in your own place, and wore a pretty dress, and had only yourself and your children to care for.

HARRIET: I don't have children.

MASTER NORCOM: But you could. Pretty ones, too.

HARRIET: Tom and I . . .

MASTER NORCOM: Shut your mouth about that boy nigger! He ain't havin' nothin' more to do with you. Now come over here. Now!

[HARRIET *steps back.*]

Why do you always cower in my presence? I am a kind man. Am I not? [*He raises his hand as if to slap her.*] Answer me?

HARRIET, MISTRESS NORCOM, AND MARY: Yes.

HARRIET: Yes sir, you are.

MASTER NORCOM: I have never forced myself upon you, and I never will.

HARRIET: Thank you sir.

MASTER NORCOM: But, you are foolish to ignore my . . . attention. Do you think you're better than the rest of them?

MARY: Sometime you act like you think you better'n the rest of us.

HARRIET: No.

MARY: You do.

HARRIET: I don't mean to.

MARY: How long you think it is 'fo he have his way by force and be through wit' you. He'd sell you down the river 'fo you could even get your drawers up.

HARRIET: That's ugly.

MARY: Life's ugly. Some of us don't get to say no.

HARRIET: Oh, Mary . . . I didn't know . . .

MARY: Jes' sayin'. . .

MASTER NORCOM: Where do you go when I'm talking to you Harriet?

HARRIET: I'm right here.

MISTRESS NORCOM: I see you there. Surely you have somethin' to attend to.

HARRIET: Yes. [*To* MASTER NORCOM] I should get back to the . . .

MASTER NORCOM: I could have any one these slave girls I want and I've chosen you. But you haven't even the sense to be grateful.

MARY: Maybe you should shut up, cooperate, and be grateful.

HARRIET: Were you?

MISTRESS NORCOM: James, we lost another field slave in birth today. Overseer says she had a White baby.

MASTER NORCOM: That's not possible. Black can't have White.

MISTRESS NORCOM: But it seems White can have Blacks all over this plantation.

HARRIET: I don't think I'm better.

MASTER NORCOM: Watch your mouth ... [*Again, the* MASTER *raises his hand as if to strike.*]

[*All three women flinch instinctively.*]

MISTRESS NORCOM: That dirty little wench, act like she thinks she's better than I.

HARRIET: Mary, I don't, I don't think I'm better. It's just my body won't let me do it. He hate us—I don't understand why he even want that. Really, I think I would be sick. He older than Grandma and smell like death.

MISTRESS NORCOM: Always lookin' like she smell something bad. Tell me, how can a slave look like that?

MASTER NORCOM: Who?

MISTRESS NORCOM: Harriet.

HARRIET: I think I hear Mistress callin'.

MASTER NORCOM [*to* HARRIET]: She's nothing for you to worry about. [*To* MISTRESS NORCOM] Surely you have distractions, something to keep your mind off of vulgar things.

HARRIET AND MISTRESS NORCOM: I think I hear the children ...

HARRIET: I should ...

MASTER NORCOM: I've ordered a house to be built down in the bottoms, behind the corn crops. You will live there, by yourself, no more visits to your grandma. I will tell the mistress and the towns-people you are there to tend to the vegetable garden and teach the slave children scripture. You will live there, and I will visit when I please. [*Beat.*] What do you have to say?

HARRIET: Only that I should die first . . .

MASTER NORCOM: "Only that I should die first," what? . . .

HARRIET: Only that I should die first, *sir.*

MASTER NORCOM: And when I visit, I shall be received with open arms.

[*Lights fade on* MISTRESS NORCOM, MASTER NORCOM, *and* MARY.]

HARRIET [*to audience*]: If I could make it all stop, but it won't.

[*The sudden sound of a violent riot is heard: windows smashing, shouts, bodies in silhouette.*]

SCENE 6

[HARRIET, MARY, *and* GRANDMA *are in Grandmother's kitchen—it has been ransacked. They stand in the middle looking at the damage.*]

HARRIET: We clean it up Grandma . . . you see . . . we'll make it all right.

GRANDMA: Ain't no "all right." I know it ain't Nat's fault . . . but Lawd . . .

MARY: Who you talkin' 'bout?

GRANDMA: Nat Turner . . .

HARRIET: He a slave what started a revolt, got *all* the White folks scared . . .

MARY: Oh . . . [MARY *starts to laugh.*] That's why Mistress been so jumpy. I jes' looked at her, an' she liked to jump outta her skin, thought she'd drop that baby right there on the floor.

HARRIET: They didn't hurt you, did they?

GRANDMA: No sweetie. They jes' take what they want, say they searchin' fo evidence of insurrection.

MARY: Insurrection?

HARRIET: Like Grandma got guns and gone go outta her head and start killin' White folks.

MARY: You think that'd be a bad idea?

[*The women begin putting the room in order.*]

GRANDMA: You shouldn't say that out loud. [*To* MARY] It's just these poor Whites, what cain't afford slaves, workin' out they anger. But it's funny, 'cause wouldn't chu think I could jes' put glass in these crackers and kill the whole damn town in one fell swoop. Come in here, eat my food while they tear up my house, lookin' for somethin' I might use to hurt them.

MARY: That's crazy.

GRANDMA: That's worse than crazy, that's stupid. Mary, get me a mop . . . Harriet, you see cain't you get these things back on the shelf . . . I gotta . . .

[*Door opens,* SAWYER *enters.*]

SAWYER: Good afternoon, ladies.

GRANDMA: Afternoon. Can I help you?

SAWYER [*to* HARRIET]: How are you this fine day, Miss Harriet?

GRANDMA: I said, can I help you?

SAWYER: Came to bring back the basket like I promised. [*Beat. Noticing the state of the place*] Perhaps I've come at an inconvenient time?

HARRIET [*taking basket*]: Thank you Massa Sawyer.

SAWYER: Please, call me Massa Samuel. Or just Samuel. [*To* GRANDMA] Came to talk to Harriet for a moment, ma'am. Jes' a minute of her time outside, I promise no harm. Maybe while we talk, you'll fill that basket up. See it comes to three dollars.

MARY: Three?!

[GRANDMA *drags* HARRIET *to the side.*]

GRANDMA: You remember what I told you.

HARRIET: Yes ma'am.

MARY [*to* SAWYER]: Maybe I can help you Massa Samuel?

SAWYER: Thank you, I'll wait for Harriet.

HARRIET [*to audience*]: Some choices not choices.

SAWYER: You like horses . . .

MARY: They all right when you need to get to someplace quick and . . .

SAWYER: You like horses, Harriet?

HARRIET [*to audience*]: Least they don't seem like choices when you're in the middle of it all. [*To* SAWYER] Yes. I do. Like horses. They're pretty and gentle and have noses like velvet. [*To audience*] Noses like velvet? [*To* SAWYER] Soft noses, that feel like . . .

SAWYER: Velvet. I agree. Got a new filly, a little chocolate and blond palomino. Maybe I can show you sometime. [*Pause.*] She's real gentle.

42

HARRIET [*to audience*]: How do I help you understand?

SAWYER: You'll come? I can drop you off at the Norcoms' after.

HARRIET [*to audience*]: Please do not think less of me.

SAWYER: Shouldn't take us a more than a few minutes out the way.

[HARRIET *lets* SAWYER *guide her out of the store. He exits as she speaks to the audience.*]

HARRIET: If I may explain. [*Beat.*] Living the life of chattel. Truly it is—indescribable. But not describing it would make our time together futile, so still I try.

[ENSEMBLE *members step forward one at a time; each offers a description to help* HARRIET *convey the realities of slavery.*]

TOM: Maybe we should tell you 'bout the plantation where they hang a slave from the ceiling.

DANIEL: They build a fire on a screen over him and put a ham on the fire.

TOM: The hot drippings fall and burn the skin of the poor victim, until he is killed or scarred forever.

HARRIET: But you see, this is not what I want tell you. None of this is new to your sensitive ears. It is how you must put your feet in the shoes of the person who has to cut the burnt man down, or in the shoes of the wife who must tend to his burns or bury him, or the children who bring him water and smell the burning flesh, so he stay alive through his torture.

CHARLOTTE: Maybe we should tell you 'bout how if you get caught stealin' once they whip you good, twice they put you in the shed and no food or water for a week, three times and they might cut off one or two fingers.

MARY: They usually leave the hand 'cause you got to have it to hold a shovel or a hoe.

HARRIET: But you've heard about that. Or at least something like it.

JOSHUA: Maybe we should tell you 'bout how they tie a third-time runner to four horses. One arm for one horse, one leg for another . . . Den they set those horses running all in different directions.

HARRIET: But again, this is not what I wish to tell you. I do not mean to upset you . . . only to help you understand. It's the niggra groomsmen who have to round up the horses and untie the victim's severed limbs. It is the wives of the groomsmen who have to hold their husbands while they tell the story at night.

GRANDMA: It's the countless women and children who must walk over the bloodstained earth to get to the fields the next day.

HARRIET: It's even the children of the master and misses who must hear the screams and witness such atrocities.

HAROLD: What you must understand is that it is in the air.

HARRIET: When there is no law that protects you. When your momma and daddy cannot protect you. When your own wits will never be a match for a life that puts you always at the mercy of others.

MARY: You can smell it.

JOSHUA: You taste it.

HAROLD: Cain't wash it off your skin. Cain't get it out your hair. It stays under your nails with the earth.

DANIEL: It is in your body and mind.

GRANDMA: It is in the soil.

MARY: In the water.

TOM: In the rags we call clothes.

CHARLOTTE: It is the way it is.

HAROLD: The way it feel from here . . .

TOM: The way it will always be . . .

MARY: And we see it . . .

TOM: And we feel it and . . .

HAROLD: We live it.

[One by one, members of the ensemble step forward, eventually obscuring HARRIET. They are singing a heartbreaking, quiet, soulful hymn.]

[HARRIET, now behind the crowd, steps forward. She is pregnant and holds a baby.]

HARRIET: And this is why you must forgive me my choice.

[Their singing is devoid of emotion and obvious sadness, for the words, and reality, are sad enough.]

[Lights fade. End Act 1.]

ACT 2

SCENE 1

[*Light rises on* MARY *and a very pregnant* HARRIET *scrubbing the floor. They take a moment to admire Harriet's baby in the Moses basket between them.*]

MARY [*talking to the baby*]: Him de hansmest thing . . . aren' chu . . . Aren'chu.

HARRIET: It's hard Mary . . . don' know sleep at all no more. Mistress all time given me the back hand if he be cryin' . . . when the milk come in, they got hard an' it hurt, an' hurt eben more when he first start to suckling.

MARY: Granny didn' help you?

HARRIET: I ain't ask.

MARY: It all bad?

HARRIET: No. Look at him. [*They gaze at the baby.*] Didn' know I could feel this way for anything. He have a holt of my heart more even den Tom did. I jes' didn't know it'd be like this.

MARY [to HARRIET]: Cain't b'lieve de mistress eben let chu stay here . . . dis baby prettier den anything she ever hab.

HARRIET: I'm sure it's not the mistress let me stay—I think the massa do, but I don' know why.

MARY: Why you don' leave de baby which yo granny?

HARRIET: Cain't.

MARY: Ya'll still ain't speakin'?

HARRIET: She think these the massa's babies.

MARY: Das what everybody think . . .

HARRIET: Not everybody. Massa knows better. Still, better Grandma think the massa forced me. I cain't have her know I laid down with Massa Samuel of my own free will . . .

MARY: Ain' nothin' 'bout you free.

HARRIET: So I cain't go near her, she look in my eyes and she know.

MARY: Why she cain't know?

HARRIET: I made her a promise, an' I broke it. 'Sides, Massa won't let me go there no more. [Beat.] He do treat me nice enuf though.

MARY: Who?

HARRIET: Babies' father.

MARY: Massa Samuel Sawyer?

HARRIET: Yes.

MARY: He treat you so good, why you still here?

[Offended, HARRIET turns her back to MARY and works on the floor.]

I didn't mean no harm. Jes' seem like he White, an' rich, an' powerful, so must be he can do whatever he want, why he not jes' come up and ride away wit' you on a horse.

HARRIET: That'd be stealin', and he cain't jes' come out an' ask Massa to sell me. You know Massa never do that. I figure now Massa see I have two, with the same father, he be so mad he'll put me on the block fo sho, den dey daddy can come buy me.

[MASTER NORCOM *enters.*]

MASTER NORCOM: Sell you fo sho, why?

[HARRIET *and* MARY *put their heads down and scrub.*]

Mary, you excuse us for minute?

MARY: Missus be on me with a switch she sees me gone.

MASTER NORCOM: Then she'll have to be on you. GO!

[MARY *runs out.* HARRIET *keeps scrubbing, instinctively protecting her pregnant belly.*]

You're still not talking to me? After I caught your little White baby? You still have nothing to say to me after I gave you a bed to rest up in for a day after the birth?

[HARRIET *stops scrubbing. She sits quietly for a long moment, finally meeting the* MASTER's *gaze.*]

HARRIET: Thank you Massa. Thank you for everything.

MASTER NORCOM: I have given you four years to come round. You think I'm gone just walk around sniffin' after you the rest of my life. You think I'm gone build you that house so some other man's

48

baby can live off of my money while you act like a White lady. You forget who you are. You forget who I am. I have no intentions of putting you on the block. I think instead I'll wait 'til you have this next and sell my new properties, together. May I? [*The* MASTER *picks up the baby in the basket and holds it carelessly.*] Mulatto slave babies bring a good price. Some little girl somewhere will be happy for a live babe to play with. Or maybe I should wait until they are eight or nine and sell them into hard labor. I just have to think about it. Perhaps it depends entirely upon how you choose to behave.

HARRIET: Please.

MASTER NORCOM: Please what Harriet?

HARRIET: Please, *sir.* My baby.

[*The* MASTER *drops the baby*—HARRIET *catches it. Lights fade as the* ENSEMBLE *sings a lullaby.*]

SCENE 2

[*Light rises on* GRANDMA.]

GRANDMA: Cookin' for de big house was a blessing an' a curse. A blessing 'cause you can feed your kids wit' de scrap, an' you always know everthin' 'bout whas happenin'. But dat's de curse too. See de massah an' missus take der breakfas in de kitchen, way from de kids, an' dat's where dey talk business an' such. An' you jes' a piece a furniture what makes de food. Dey be sayin' things like, "Gotta cow on de Avery plantation I had ta order put down, she too ol', and, speakin' a old, Jessie gettin' up there an' ain't been pickin' his quota, you know Jessie?" An' de missus say, "You know I cain't hardly tell any de niggas apart, specially not them blue-black field hands," an' de massah say, "Well, don't know if it's bettah to have Jim Perkins ride him harder, if I make more to sell him at a loss, or maybe best we put him out all our misery." An' I gotta say, "You wan' mo gravy fo yo biscuits ma'am? Sir?"

[HARRIET *enters. No longer pregnant, she carries a toddler strapped to her back and now an infant strapped to her front. She's dressed to run. She addresses the audience.*]

HARRIET: Perhaps my enslaved comrades did not visit thoughts of running as often as I . . . though it is hard to imagine one wouldn't. Every bush, every rock, gully, or tree seems to offer shelter for an unplanned escape. But they are hollow offerings, as nature has provided little protection from the noses of the hounds and the ruthless desperation of hungry slave catchers. The night I birthed my girl, the master made clear his intentions to no longer torment me with threats. That he should not only make good on his promises, but sell my children as far away as possible. This drove me finally to run.

[*In silhouette the audience sees a depiction of* HARRIET's *escape, helped by the* ENSEMBLE.]

[*A light rises on* HARRIET *standing in Grandma's doorway, severely disheveled and feverish.* GRANDMA *goes to her and pulls her in. They hug.* GRANDMA *rocks* HARRIET *as she clings to her and sobs. Lights fade.*]

[*Light rises on* DANIEL.]

DANIEL: I wan' show you sumpin I carry wif' me. Is what dey call a bill o' sale fo my daddy. Dat's de papers go wit' you when you get put on de block. Fount it in a box under my mama's bed when she past. Cain't read, but I knowed some o' what it say, my mama knowed it, tolt it to me. Say some'n 'bout dis here niggra, Moses, solt to

so's and so, on such 'n' such a date fo de 'mount of sebbenty-fibe
dollars, an' dis here de part I like: It say—Moses, a strong buck wif'
a good manner, dark-black skin, an' good teef. Put it in dis pouch
wear roun' my neck, make me feel close to him.

SCENE 3

[*Light rises on* HARRIET *holding a baby, another in a basket at her feet.*
GRANDMA *tends to* HARRIET's *many bites and abrasions. She places a
damp cloth over a snake bite on her leg.*]

GRANDMA: You lucky it wasn't a cottonmouth . . .

HARRIET: Ow . . .

GRANDMA: You still feverish . . . I think it's infection, not venom. This
should draw it out.

HARRIET: I shouldn't have put the babies through it, Grandma, the
mosquitoes were worse than the snakes . . .

GRANDMA: . . . And the babies didn't cry?

HARRIET: Not once.

GRANDMA: Thas a miracle.

HARRIET: Well, I give each a finger dipped in honey an' moonshine, hid
in the marshes, but my milk was dryin' up fast. I even thought
'bout runnin' to Tom, but I was scared of the paddy rollers and the
overseers . . .

GRANDMA: Ya shoulda been more scared of Tom's wife than the overseers . . .

HARRIET [*chuckling*]: I thought of that too.

[*They sit in silence for a moment.* HARRIET *puts the baby to her breast.*]

GRANDMA: Harriet. You would run and not come say bye to your old granny?

HARRIET: I thought better that than you know the truth.

GRANDMA: Girl, I saw the truth coming minute that Massa Samuel walk in here talkin' 'bout, "Whas your name . . . ?"

HARRIET: I promised.

GRANDMA: I was wrong to ask you to. Grandma know how it be, an' I sorry. I so sorry I ask more of you than the world let you be. You a good girl 'cause you got a good heart, an' a good mind, an' what between those strong legs of yours, an' who go there don' make you less.

HARRIET: What I gone do?

[*The men in the* ENSEMBLE *sing a work song as they set up the shed from the top of the play.*]

GRANDMA: You cain't stay here, this the first place they come lookin'. I been thinkin' on this. I know how you don't much like tight places. But there a little space, right under the rafters, behind the chimney, up in the shed. You hide up there. Jes' for a spell. Jes' 'til he get tired of lookin' for you an' we figure out how we get you North.

HARRIET: Me and the babies?

GRANDMA: You know you cain't run with two babies.

HARRIET: You right, but I cain't run without them—they a piece of me.

GRANDMA: Then seems you have a choice to make. But you best be thinkin' 'bout that where you safe from harm. Now that you decided to start runnin' you cain't go back . . .

HARRIET: An' I wouldn't, not for nothin'.

[*Lights fade. The house servant's work rhythms from earlier blend with the rhythms of the workers in the cotton field as they build Harriet's hiding place.*]

[HARRIET *hands* GRANDMA *her babies.* GRANDMA *exits with them.* HARRIET *is alone. She climbs into her hiding space.*]

[*Blackout.*]

SCENE 4

[*Light rises on* ISAAC.]

ISAAC: Hadn't nebber seen dis kind a place 'fore I come here. Worked for the Montgomerys two counties over. They like most White folks: a small house, a shed, an' two or three of us in a back room offa de kitchen. We's all hungry all de time, not jes' us what work there, but the White folks what owns us too. Three years past, a drought kills off the Montgomerys' wheat crop. First they sell my four-year-ol' girl, then three o' the five chickens, then my woman, then the mule what pulled de plow. I can pull good as the mule *an'* use my hands. I don' get solt here, 'til affer de Montgomerys' baby dies when de missus' milk dry up. It better here . . . don't know hunger no more, an' always hab shoes on my feet.

[*Light fades on* ISAAC *and rises on* HARRIET *from her hiding space.*]

HARRIET: There is a blinding darkness. Darker than the brightest, whitest light. A deafening silence that can hurt your ears with its complete absence of sound. And this is how it was. It is small, but, even on the worse days, it is bigger than my world outside. This space bigger even than my world ever was or could be. An' maybe there's room to breathe in the North, but maybe I cain't breathe without my children. Maybe this air will taint them more if I ain't here to protect them . . . This is how it was. And this is how it felt. And this not something easy to tell you.

[*Light changes; it is as though Harriet's hiding space is illuminated from within.*]

[GRANDMA *pokes her head in.*]

GRANDMA: You awake?

HARRIET: Always.

GRANDMA: You keep stretchin' those legs?

HARRIET: Best I can Grandma. How are the children?

GRANDMA: They sleep. Send me down your waste.

[HARRIET *lowers a large bucket on a rope. Through the following* GRANDMA *exchanges it for a basket of provisions and a fresh bucket.*]

HARRIET: Joseph minding you? Louisa, she eating? You know how she get funny 'bout eating, it worry me she won't have enough fat on her bones to keep her warm through winter . . .

GRANDMA: They fine sweetie. How you feel?

HARRIET: Back hurt . . . But good Grandma. Truly. Maybe I stay here forever . . . I like Master think I ran North, an' I right here under his nose.

GRANDMA: I don' like this playin' with fire.

HARRIET: Grandma, I need your help . . .

54

GRANDMA: What I been doin' all these months?

HARRIET: I been thinkin' on it an' I know what to do . . . I need several sheets of parchment paper and sealing wax . . . [*beat*] an', this the part you not gone like . . . I need you get Massa Samuel to come by . . .

GRANDMA: Here?

HARRIET: I know . . . but I must speak with him. Please, just get him to agree to come by after sundown, don' tell him I here, jes' bring him an' I will explain everything . . . [GRANDMA *does not respond.*] You say you trust I have a good head, then trust me this. I will not be found out; I will not bring harm to you or the children. But I cannot leave them.

GRANDMA: You readin' that Bible I brung you?

HARRIET: I usin' it.

[GRANDMA's *sent up the new provisions and begins to exit.*]

GRANDMA: I see you maybe day after tomorrow. Try, please, to move them bowels.

[GRANDMA *exits.*]

HARRIET: I learned to read on the Bible. Not so exciting as my love and adventure stories, but it's a nice book to have read. I pray God understand how I use it now. The pages where I write, to keep my head out places where it ought not to be, and still my mind make the voices come . . .

MASTER NORCOM: I can smell you up there Harriet . . .

HARRIET: So I write . . .

MASTER NORCOM: Used to smell good, now I wouldn't want to touch you for the stench of that smell . . .

HARRIET: And I write . . .

MASTER NORCOM: The missus say she miss you. Say she ain't got no one to fill her mind with murderous thoughts. That keep her under my feet an' so, I miss you too.

HARRIET: Shut it! [MASTER NORCOM *disappears.*] I tried writing stories for the children . . . but since Granny cain't read to 'em, that seem a waste of time and a little sad. So I write 'bout what I know. What I remember, way I want it to be, way I hope it be someday.

[HARRIET *writes.*]

SCENE 5

[HARRIET's *writing.* TOM *appears out of nowhere in his own light.*]

TOM: Whatchu doin'?

HARRIET: Tom . . . you scared me. [*Beat.*] Writing.

TOM: May I?

[HARRIET *hands* TOM *the book.* MASTER NORCOM *reappears.*]

MASTER NORCOM: I can smell you Harriet.

TOM: You want I kill him for you Harriet?

HARRIET: Thank you Tom, that'd be very thoughtful.

[MASTER NORCOM's *light goes out.*]

TOM: Says here you loved me more than you knew to tell me.

HARRIET: Yes.

TOM: Says, if you could, you would tell me now jes' how much.

HARRIET: Yes Tom. I sorry I didn' know how to say it plain before.

TOM: Why you love me? Jes' 'cause I can read your words?

HARRIET: No, Tom. I love you understand my words. I love you listen, and so you hear my words, and so you hear my heart. I love your brown hard arms, I love the hair on your chest, an' the way your neck smell. I love the way I have to stand on my toes to smell that neck.

TOM: Thas real nice Harriet. You got anyone else you need kilt today?

HARRIET: No. Not today. Thank you.

[TOM's *light fades.*]

    [*To* TOM] Wait Tom . . . wait . . .

[TOM's *light rises subtly.*]

TOM: Uh huh . . .

HARRIET: Why you love me?

TOM: For your beauty an' your innate kindness.

HARRIET [*to audience*]: Afraid as I was of being discovered . . . my greatest fear was that I should come out of hiding without my mind.

[GRANDMA *enters.*]

GRANDMA: Harriet . . .

HARRIET: Tom?

GRANDMA: It's Grandma . . . Sorry I ain't been to see you for a while . . . come down for a moment and stretch those legs . . . Got the chillun playin' on the front porch with Mary, leff the door open an' tells 'em I be right back, jes' goin' to put on the potatoes fo dinner.

[HARRIET *climbs down.*]

I worry 'bout you up there all the time mumblin'. You really thought I might be Tom . . . ?

HARRIET: 'Course not, I was mostly half-asleep.

GRANDMA: Massa Sawyer roun' back . . . you want I bring him in?

HARRIET: Yes ma'am.

[SAWYER *emerges from a shadow.*]

SAWYER: Harriet?

HARRIET: Massa Samuel.

SAWYER: You don't look well . . .

HARRIET [*to* GRANDMA]: We'll be all right Grandma . . .

[GRANDMA *exits.*]

Forgive me please . . . lately I not so sure whas really happenin' an' what's happenin' my mind. You here?

SAWYER: I am. The word spoken about town is you ran North . . .

HARRIET: I intend that be the word, an' I need your help . . .

SAWYER: I bought your children. They are with your grandmother . . .

HARRIET: Thank you . . . for purchasing [*beat*] my children. I am in need of a favor.

SAWYER: Knowing you are here places me in the precarious position of harboring a fugitive . . . I do not feel at all comfortable.

HARRIET: Yes. I too am, uncomfortable. I must request a favor. I beg that you help me—perhaps in remembrance of pleasant times we have spent together . . .

SAWYER: I am here; you may as well make the request.

HARRIET: I have written several letters—I have addressed them from myself to my former master . . .

SAWYER: Legally you are still . . .

HARRIET: Of course . . . my master . . . I only ask that you take these letters on your travels North and from time to time mail them to Master Norcom as though they are from me.

SAWYER: I have always admired your cleverness . . .

HARRIET: I think you have, on occasion, been amused by my cleverness . . .

SAWYER: I shall do this . . .

HARRIET: Thank you.

SAWYER: Take care of yourself, Harriet.

[SAWYER *exits.*]

HARRIET [*muttering to herself*]: "Take care of yourself, Harriet." "Harriet, you take care of yourself." Yes Master . . . I be sure do that . . . be sure to "take care" of myself because that is what I have always done. I "take care" of myself.

[*Light rises abruptly on* MARY.]

MARY: Once I cleanin' up de lil missus room.

HARRIET: An' the voices don' stop . . .

[HARRIET *exits to hiding space.*]

MARY: I sebben. She nine. She come in an' say, "Whatchu doin'?" An' I
say, "Cleanin' your room," an' she say, "Why?" an' I say, " 'Cause
my mama ask me to," an' she say, "Uh uh, you cleanin' my room
'cause you blong to me like my toys." An' then she say, "Anything
I ask you to do you have to do it, 'cause you belong to me." An'
truly I din' know what she talkin' 'bout so I say, "You need to
move so's I can finish my work," and she slap me, hard, an' den she
start to cry, an' her mama come in, and an' she say, "Mary won' do
like I ask," an' her mama call my mama, make her turn me over
her knee, bare my bottom an' beat me wiff de hair side a brush 'til
I bleed. Dat's de firs time I got a real wuppin'. Still didn' understand what she meant by, "I own you." Still don' quite understand
how someone can say dey own me when dey not God.

[HARRIET *has reappeared.* MARY'*s focus shifts from the house to*
HARRIET.]

Harriet, I still here. Harriet?

HARRIET: Mary, I sorry.

[MARY'*s light out.* MASTER NORCOM'*s rises.*]

MASTER NORCOM: I can smell you up there, Harriet.

HARRIET: Didn't Tom kill you?

MASTER NORCOM: That was a while ago now. I'm back. And I can
smell you.

HARRIET: No.

MASTER NORCOM: I most certainly can.

HARRIET: 'Cause you like a dog. 'Cause you like a bloodhound.

MASTER NORCOM: Careful how you speak to me. Even in your mind I can crush you and your little bastard porch monkeys.

HARRIET: No! No! No! In my mind, you are nothing but a sad little man. Not even man enough to convince a slave girl to be with you. An' how hard could it be really? Look at me. You own me. I can't even claim my own fingernails, and you sniff round me actin' jealous and foolish . . . [MASTER NORCOM's *light goes out.* HARRIET *hears the children's singing, for the first time.*] Children? Children!

[*Pause. To audience*] In the dark, there is time to think, an' remember . . .

[*Lights rise on* SAWYER, MASTER NORCOM, *and* TOM.]

SAWYER, MASTER NORCOM, AND TOM: You the prettiest little Black thing I ever laid my eyes on.

HARRIET: Tom?

TOM: Harriet.

HARRIET: Samuel?

SAWYER: I say, you the prettiest little Black thing I ever laid my eyes on.

HARRIET: Why I cain't jes' be the prettiest little thing? Why it got to be a Black before it. You tell White gals, dey de prettiest little White gals?

SAWYER AND MASTER NORCOM: Why not jest take a compliment as it's given?

HARRIET: Didn' you kill him Tom?

TOM: I did.

[MASTER NORCOM's *light goes out.*]

SAWYER: I say, why not just take the compliment.

HARRIET: Why not give a compliment right?

SAWYER: Harriet, someday you will learn to watch your mouth round the people who mean you well.

HARRIET: Tom . . .

TOM: Harriet?

HARRIET: You let him talk to me this way?

TOM: No dear Harriet . . . I kill him too if you like . . .

[SAWYER's *lights goes out.*]

HARRIET [*to audience*]: When it's too cold or too hot, or I am especially scared . . . the voices don' say what I need them to . . .

TOM: I heard you have two half-breeds.

HARRIET: It's true. You seen them? How they look?

TOM: I hear they ain't the master's.

HARRIET: It would be better for you if they were?

TOM: Maybe.

HARRIET: I hear things too Tom, an' I hear you settled down with a house girl from your own plantation. You have a likin' for house girls Tom?

TOM: I loved you.

HARRIET: But you didn't come back.

TOM: He took our future, and he burned it, and what was I to say to you 'bout that? How was I to explain that I gave myself up for you, and it got burned, and there ain't nothing left. That little gal I married don't know me, Harriet. She has half a man, and that's all she'll ever have, 'cause that's all that's left. But, for her, half a man is enough. For you, you deservin' of a full man.

HARRIET: You shoulda come . . .

TOM: You shouldna laid down with a White man.

[MASTER NORCOM's *light rises.*]

MASTER NORCOM: I can smell you up there, Harriet.

HARRIET: You need to get out my head.

[TOM's *light fades.*]

    Not you!

[TOM's *light rises.*]

MASTER NORCOM: I can smell you up there . . .

HARRIET: YOU!

[MASTER NORCOM's *light goes out.*]

    Or maybe that's not how it goes. Maybe it goes more like this, yes, this is how I make it go . . .

TOM: You all right up in that tight space?

HARRIET: No, Tom, it hurts.

TOM: I'm sorry. I truly wish I could ease your pain.

HARRIET: Thank you.

TOM: Saw your babies playing in the yard. They pretty. Look like they mama.

HARRIET: Thank you, Tom.

TOM: I miss you, Harriet.

HARRIET: I miss you, Tom, always will.

TOM: When we escape to the North together . . .

[TOM's *light goes out.*]

HARRIET: And that's as far as I can . . . So, mostly, I think and dream of my children. Grandma told me to try to protect my heart, to love my children only as much as is necessary, but no more. I know she knows this is impossible. I make a sharp tool with the handle of my slop bucket and bore a little hole in the wall here. I can look out and see them in the yard. First they babies, tied round they middles with string to the clothesline so they not wander far. I see my boy eat dirt, an' I cain't say nothin'. I see my baby girl poke my boy in the eye, an' he cry, an' she laugh. I see dem later, bigger, make figures on the groun' with dirt. I want to help them make letters. I see Granma scoop them up an' take them in to dinner. I see puffs of hair turn into long braids with ribbon . . . I see them growing, strong and happy and healthy. Seven years I watch them grow an' can't touch them.

[*The children's voices are heard (and may be played by* ENSEMBLE *members—for example those who play* MARY *and* DANIEL *or* ISAAC*). The children are not seen through the following.*]

LOUISA: Mama. I knowed you come back.

HARRIET: You *knew* I'd come back.

LOUISA: Das what I said. I *knowed* you come back. And here you is.

HARRIET: Yes. Here I *is*.

JOSEPH: You bring us presents?

HARRIET: Yes, baby boy. Sure did.

JOSEPH: You bring us candy?

HARRIET: All the candy you want forever.

LOUISA: We don' wan' no candy—we jes' want you to stay.

HARRIET: Always. I always be right here. Right here where you can run to when you need me. An' I protect you, an' I keep you safe, an' I keep you warm. An' you only have to answer to me.

JOSEPH: I thought we only have to answer to God.

HARRIET: You only have to answer to God and me.

LOUISA: I love you, Mama.

HARRIET: I love you too, baby. [*To* JOSEPH] What about you?

JOSEPH: I cain't say that. Don' wan' sound like a girl. But you is a good mama.

HARRIET: I *am* a good mama.

JOSEPH: Granny say it not good to flatter yourself.

HARRIET: An' that's as far as I can imagine it . . . or I will scream. Or die.

[GRANDMA *enters. She sets down a basket of food and a slop jar.*]

GRANDMA: You won't die.

HARRIET: Grandma? That you? You real?

GRANDMA: Who else it be? How I not be real? An', don' be talkin' 'bout dyin'.

HARRIET: All these years. Maybe death be better.

GRANDMA: You choose death, the master wins. You decided this where you need to be . . . Come down here, Granny need to talk to your face.

HARRIET: It's near day Granny, you think it safe?

GRANDMA: None of this never was safe . . . Come down here, I'll check your head for lice while we talk. [*While* HARRIET *leaves her space,* GRANDMA *speaks.*] Mary missin' you. Come over here talkin' 'bout how she think even the missus wish you was there 'cause things at the house so slow an' boring now. Says she take care of the chilluns in the big house now, an' they be askin' after you all the time.

[HARRIET *has emerged and settles, painfully, on the floor by* GRANDMA. GRANDMA *begins parting and examining the hair.*]

HARRIET: I been up there a long time, Grandma.

GRANDMA: Too long baby.

HARRIET: Got another letter for Massa Samuel.

GRANDMA: Girl . . .

HARRIET: I even wrote in it fo Massa Norcom to tell you I's OK.

GRANDMA: You sure this all part of your plan an' not just pride?

HARRIET: It true, I'm prideful of outsmarting Massa Norcom, but also it seem like a good way to go 'bout it. Let me read you the letter: "Dear Master Norcom, I surely hope God and you and de missus can forgive me. I ran 'cause my bein' there ain't helpin' the fambly. I's sorry I had dem babies outta wedlock an' I ain't a good example to set for the chilluns . . ." But this the part I like this part best . . . I write . . . "I do hope your investment in bounty hunters does not drain your family's resources. Might I suggest you donate those funds to the church coffers, or even allow Mistress Norcom a new dress, as I will not be found."

GRANDMA: I hate see you anger him so . . .

HARRIET [*amused*]: Do you really Granny?

GRANDMA [*laughing*]: . . . No . . . It makes me quite proud. [*Beat.*] It seems there's more Massa Sam could do to make it easier for you.

HARRIET: You knew he wouldn't. [*Beat.*] Grandma, I ain't fifteen no more. I did think he was special then. Really, I did. He was kind, and seem like he the only man I was gone be with an' not feel like I break into pieces. Think I even made myself call it love. Prob'ly deep inside I didn't never really think he was gone carry me off on a horse an' make me the first niggra mistress of a plantation. Didn' wanna be first Negro mistress. I jes' needed a place to rest my head and put my heart and put my hopes, an' he there, an' he not the doctor, an' I cain't have Tom, an' I think, God forgive me, I would do it again.

GRANDMA: Hush girl, you ain't got to splain. [*Beat.*] It's been too long. I think even Mary get suspicious; she come by an' all the time I be comin' from the shed. Yesterday, she even say, "Seem like you go out there more'n you used to. Seem like I may be not the only one will notice that."

HARRIET: That mighty clever for Mary.

GRANDMA: She a bright girl. Ain't been hidin' in a crawl space for seven years.

HARRIET: Grandma!

GRANDMA: We both know it's time. [*Long beat.*] I worked out passage for you on a ship what sails North. Cap'n a good White man, always like your Granny an' do us this favor for a small fortune.

HARRIET: I won' see my babies again.

GRANDMA: They ain't babies no more. The way you see them now makin' you feel better? You die up here or lose your senses, they still won' have a mama . . . an' God forbid you found out, an' we all put in jail or worse.

HARRIET: They good kids ain't they?

GRANDMA: Yes.

HARRIET: They gone be good people?

GRANDMA: Yes.

HARRIET: They gone be safe an' happy an' healthy?

GRANDMA: Might be.

HARRIET: You think one day they be free.

GRANDMA: They free now.

HARRIET: Not long as Massa Sam got papers on them. He marry the wrong kind or get thrown from a horse, an' they be on the block tomorrow . . .

GRANDMA: I almost got the money to buy them outright. They gone be all right.

HARRIET: No such thing as all right in this place.

GRANDMA: You been talkin' to God since you been up there?

HARRIET: I pray. Sometime I think he even listen . . . But sometime I think I don't know who I'm talkin' to.

GRANDMA: You jes' know this. People long 'fore you, people now, people years after you be lost an' sufferin', an' it don't mean cain't find a private peace in the middle of it. [*Beat.*] Oh Lord, I been gone too long. You get yourself ready.

HARRIET: Yes ma'am.

[GRANDMA *exits. The* ENSEMBLE *hums a lullaby. The children climb into the hiding space with* HARRIET. *They cuddle in. They are, in that moment, for that time, reunited, the lighting indicates night turning into day.* HARRIET *whispers over the sleeping children to the audience.*]

And Grandma gave me a special gift. She let me spend my last hours in hiding with the children, being careful not to tell them where I was going. I discover that my brave little Joseph knew where his momma was from the time he was five. While playing in the yard with a friend, my boy heard me sneeze. My angel kept it to himself, away from his sister an' Grandma, steering friends to a different part of the yard whenever they played. It is unusual and devastating the way slavery makes men of our boys and women of our girls. I hold this thought close. I hold the voices, the stories, the atrocities, and indignities next to my heart, close to my soul, and climb out of my hiding place into a future only slightly more secure.

[HARRIET *untangles herself from the sleeping children, giving each a last kiss and covering them with the blankets. The* ENSEMBLE *emerges from the back and takes up the hymn. Eventually it will morph into an uplifting song of freedom.*]

I have always wanted to think that things happen for a reason. It comforts me to think that maybe horrible things happen so that they will never happen again. But no, that is too easy. I think horrible things happen because they do. But I do believe that we find a way. That we are human, and so we must find a way. And it gets better until it gets worse, and it gets better again and sometimes a little worse and, maybe later, better even than that. My hiding place was small, but, in it, my soul was able to soar. In it, even when my body hurt more than I have the words to describe, I was more free than any bill of sale would ever make me. I did find my way North. Eventually my grown children even made their way to me . . . I found a life rich with the joys and sorrows of, a life. But it was above Grandmother's shed, in the cold and the dark, in the heat and the solitude, that I found my voice . . . so that my voice might find its way into the world . . . In that tight, dark place my mind grew, my heart expanded, and, with a pen and scraps of paper, I was able to stretch my arms out . . .

[ENSEMBLE *members have gathered around her and have begun singing a rousing, hopeful spiritual. It is not a celebration; it is an affirmation of life.* HARRIET *stands still. She is not triumphant; there is not happiness. There is rather the conviction of one who will survive, the satisfaction of one who will tell her story, the need to know that she has been heard. She walks upstage into the deep-blue sky of the future.*]

[*Lights fade on all. End of play.*]